Beyond Interpretation

Beyond Interpretation

Studies in the Modern Short Story

Daniel Burke, FSC

The Whitston Publishing Company
Troy, New York
1991

Copyright 1991
Daniel Burke FSC

Library of Congress Catalog Card Number
 90-70718

ISBN 0–87875–394–X
Printed in the United States of America

For Ben Bernstein

*Words, once my stock, are wanting to commend
So great a man and so good a friend.*

Table of Contents

Preface	ix
Introduction: Assumptions and Methods	3
James Joyce: Gabriel and the Women of "The Dead"	27
D.H. Lawrence: The Secrets of "The Rocking-Horse Winner"	49
Katherine Mansfield: Mansfield's "Fly" and the Vulnerable Boss	65
Katherine Anne Porter: The Contentment of María Concepción	79
William Faulkner: Praise and Learning in the Short Version of "The Bear"	103
Ernest Hemingway: Nick's "Big Two-Hearted River"	121
Flannery O'Connor: Pride and Prejudice in "The Artificial Nigger"	145
Eudora Welty: "Powerhouse" and the Mystery of Art	163

Preface

Literary theories in recent decades have become unusually diverse and competitive. Whether they have addressed the production or the reception of literary texts, the meaning or special use of language in these works, their social and historical contexts, the theories evolved have been elaborate and detailed, especially when the procedures of other disciplines like linguistics and psychology have been employed. Moreover, their basic assumptions have, at times, been quite radical. There has been much to satisfy the modern taste for novelty.

What these developments have often obscured is the place of modern theories in the long tradition since Plato. However, as monographs on individual theories have appeared and, more recently, surveys like Vincent Leitch's *American Literary Criticism from the Thirties to the Eighties* (1988), it emerges that the newest ideas, not surprisingly, had anticipations and counterparts in the earlier tradition. It has been observed, too, that basic academic work, like undergraduate teaching, has been only slightly affected by newer theories, if at all. This result may be attributed to the increasing complexity of the theories themselves, to their lagging application in practical criticism, to the failure of any one theory or related criticism to dominate the field as did New Criticism, say, in the forties and fifties.

At this juncture, then, it may be that we will simply wait for a new theory that will command wider adherence and will effect more basic changes in criticism or in teaching. What is less likely is that theory would return to an earlier stage where teaching or criticism have in effect settled. But a middle way might suggest a synthesis of various modern theories in a wider framework, traditional or not. Or, in a more limited fashion, it might lead to a re-examination of specific elements in the tradition in the light of recent theories. For a contemporary theorist can never fully escape the general issues and concerns of his or her predecessors, and, on the other hand, we cannot fully understand a new contribution (or judge its value for the future) until we understand how it is like and unlike related concepts of the past.

The present book attempts to maintain the double perspective of this last approach. What I am concerned with basically is the perennial but intractable problem of the meaning of a literary text and what lies beyond (or within) its meaning in the way of aesthetic value. The problem was set by Aristotle when he discussed the sources of poetry in the human desire to know and in a basic sense of harmony (*Poetics*, 4). The most popular setting of the problem was for centuries in the off-handed and latitudinarian remark of Horace that poets aim either to benefit, or to amuse, or to utter words at once both pleasing and helpful to life (*Art of Poetry*, 333-34). But, despite millennia of discussion in the West, the problematic relationship of profitable meaning to harmony and amusement has yet to achieve a widely accepted solution.

My approach to the problem here is both theoretical and critical. The introduction describes my basic assumptions about the problem of meaning and value in terms of traditional grammatical and rhetorical meaning being structured further by internally required, fit relations. My attempt is to take that

Preface xi

concept several steps beyond modern formalist and structuralist versions, though not in deconstructive or other post-structuralist fashion. The application, thereafter, is to a selection of modern British and American short stories that share a common excellence but vary considerably in the way it is achieved. Here the emphasis *is* critical not biographical (on the development of the individual writers) or historical (on the development of the genre itself). The critical essays, then, are efforts at synthesis and reorientation. They are not meant to establish some new, undetected meaning in the stories, but rather to assess and balance existing interpretations in holistic treatments while also suggesting some of the internally generated ways the stories are crafted as works of art.

And the effort at synthesis is needed, for the tide of interpretations has increased considerably. Textbooks and manuals over the years have provided brief analyses of stories as they introduced students to the constituent parts of narrative, as in Cleanth Brooks and Robert Penn Warren's *Understanding Fiction* (1943), or as they surveyed the history of the genre, as in Ray West and Robert Stallman's *The Art of Modern Fiction* (1949). There has also been a growing supply of substantial articles for scholars and teachers in a variety of journals like *Studies in Short Fiction*, articles often focused on a single theme or motif, but usually offering some light on the daunting complexity of a good story and the mystery of how it has been constructed. And now increasingly there are monographs on the short stories of individual authors, of different periods, or with particular themes. What has been lacking, however, have been convenient syntheses of this accumulating scholarship for individual stories.

Examples are offered here from eight authors: James Joyce, D. H. Lawrence, Katherine Mansfield, Katherine Anne Porter, William Faulkner, Ernest Hemingway, Flannery O'Connor, and

Eudora Welty. Needless to say, a broader coverage would have attended to others: John Updike and John Cheever certainly, if not also V. S. Pritchett, Frank O'Connor, J. F. Powers or a half-dozen others. For each of those I do treat, I have chosen one of their more popular stories, one which I believed represented major achievement in general ("The Dead") or had some interesting, if flawed, development of one element of the narrative ("The Fly").

My thanks are due to Mary Anne Lutz for important ideas about two of the stories; to Joseph Wiesenfarth, James Kincaid, John Keenan, Barbara Millard, and Richard Tiedeken for reading several chapters and offering valuable suggestions; to Lawrence Oelschlegel, F.S.C., for giving some consistency to my punctuation and phrasing. I am especially grateful to the National Endowment for the Humanities, to La Salle University, and to the Christian Brothers' Community there, for leaves and grants that provided time for the work.

Beyond Interpretation

Studies in the Modern Short Story

Introduction: Assumptions and Methods

Over the century and a half since it began, the art of the short story has had notable achievements, yet it has remained a modest and, in some ways, a mysterious craft. In its popular forms, it has had wide distribution; in its artistic forms, it has engaged impressive efforts of major writers. But, as it has now become conventional to say, the genre as a whole has been strangely neglected by publishers, scholars, and the reading public. Some pessimists even announce its imminent demise, much as they have regularly scheduled the disappearance of the short story's older sibling, the novel. But, as Nadine Gordimer has observed, "Like a child suffering from healthy neglect, the short story survives."

Indeed it often thrives, sustained simply by our enormous appetite for story. In our times, it competes well with radio, movies, and films, even as it contributes to those media and suffers the loss of its own print vehicles, like the popular magazines of recent decades. In academe, however, theories about its specific character are still very thin; none has had general acceptance.[1] The interesting paradox is that, even after considerable study of the short story, we have only fragmentary notions of what the genre itself is. We typically begin with the briefest of descriptions—our genre is the "short prose narrative fiction"—but even lengthy discussion does not get us much beyond that.[2] We feel, nevertheless, that this literary kind has other specific differences from the novel and the novella, in one direction, and, in the other, from several types of short prose tales, some of which go back to antiquity. But we seem left with a rather large and baggy class, a grouping somewhere between the much larger class of narrative as such and the many smaller genres of the short story itself—the initiation story, the detective, the lyric-epiphany, and so on. For it is difficult to pin down more specific characteristics on the basis, say, of the sound structure or determinate length often involved in genre definitions (fourteen lines of iambic pentameter with designated rime schemes for the sonnet, but only "prose" and the very flexible "brief" for the short story) or of approaches to topic or narrator's style as in "detective story parody" (indicating a specific subject matter, a tone, and a technique, but only "narrative" and "fiction" for the short story itself).[3]

It may be, of course, that we want too much from a genre definition of the short story. For what any such definition usually offers is only a set of conventions and fashions within which writers pursue their more basic job of creating an artistic work and readers interpret it. It is not surprising, then, to find that notes which at one time or another have been proposed by Edgar Allan Poe, Brander Matthews and others as characteristic only of the short story—"closeness of texture," "freedom from excrescence," "unity of effect"—should apply in due measure to all literary works. On the other hand, the term "fiction" in the usual definition of the short story seems often to imply literary value, too. But, while we recognize them as fictions, neither the ancient didactic parable nor the dramatized advertisements of modern television strike us as particularly artistic. Should we not say, then, that the notable short stories we are to deal with here, with as much attention as possible to their artistic values, are "brief *literary* and fictional narratives in prose"?

That string of terms gets a bit awkward, of course, and "literary" opens a Pandora's box—even if we prefer the version of the myth that makes it a box of blessings as well as curses. In any event, I want to deal with the notion of literary value at some length here, as I attempt to spell out as clearly as possible the assumptions governing my analyses. But I do not want to circumvent the immediate difficulties of "brief." For I believe that valuable insights into the *practice* of the short story can be derived from considering the implications of its brevity, of how individual writers pursue their tasks of creating a narrator, plot, characters, settings, and themes and unify these parts under the special limitation. But whether a character changes or not, whether there is one episode or several, whether the matter dealt with be a fragment or larger slice of life, a passing mood or a settled attitude—these variables seem part of the great variety offered by narrative itself, not fundamental characteristics of the short story as such.[4] Again, it may be that particular choices in such matters characterize the structure of one or another story, the style of one or another writer, the fashion of one or another period. But such features seem to be neither essentials of the short story genre as such nor necessary sources of literary value in individual stories.

Likewise, we can note the possible influence on the first short story writers of eighteenth century character sketches, essays, or the chatty narrators of novels. We might be tempted, then, to think that what differentiates their work in the new form from earlier prose tales is that they develop plot, characters, and other cumulative parts more optimally in each case and get them into better balance in a short narrative. But if indeed they do not now flatten out other elements when they stress a fully developed setting in "Rip Van Winkle" or a psychologically convincing narrator-character in "Tell-Tale Heart" or symbolically developed themes in "Young Goodman Brown" and "Bartleby," the notions of "optimal development" and "better balance" are clearly matters of literary value itself, rather than of generic requirements analogous to "fourteen lines of iambic pentameter."

So I think we must be content with a relatively simple notion about the kind of work addressed here—the brief literary and fictional narrative in prose—and get on to the happily more rewarding business of analysis, of seeing how stories are put together and what this tells us about their values. Specifically, I want to reconsider some of the classics of the modern short story, from James Joyce to Eudora Welty. But what I want to show particularly is that a sustained analysis of structural relationships in these quite different stories is not only feasible but is centrally important to their evaluation. While the structure and value I am concerned with here, and will ultimately suggest are identical, have not been developed in these stories as mechanically as Mr. Poe suggests with his term "pre-established," I think we can accept his description of the end result:

> In the whole composition there should be no word written, of which the tendency, direct or indirect, is not to the one pre-established design. And by such means, with such care and skill, a picture is at length painted which leaves in the mind of him who contemplates it with a kindred art, a sense of the fullest satisfaction.[5]

At its best, criticism is an advanced stage of that "kindred art," the art of seeing how every element contributes to the final effect of a good story. Literary critics, that is, engage in that reflex operation in which initial understanding and judgment of a text are further evaluated in the light of additional, relevant knowledge. Deeper knowledge of the text is involved, but there is also the critic's familiarity with similar works and their history and with theory.[6]

It is fair to say, however, that literary criticism has usually been preoccupied with its interpretive work.[7] It has often, at least in its academic form, neglected the work of evaluation. It was not surprising, then, that some twenty years ago, Susan Sontag should protest the endless accumulation of interpretations and call for a criticism that "would serve the work of art, not usurp its place," one which would have "more extended and thorough descriptions of *form* . . . the luminousness of the thing in itself."[8] Miss Sontag's call represents a recurrent aspiration in the history of criticism but one which has not often had a sustained or systematic response. Modern structuralists, new critics, and others, of course, have maintained that this is precisely what they have been about. But neither the distillation of ultimate paradoxes, the winnowing of repeated meanings to suggest the "density" of a communication, or other refinements of meaning as such, seem often to approach "the luminousness of the thing itself."

In any event, it is to that most difficult, not to say intractable, value that I have attempted to order the present analyses. My contention is that one can at least suggest ways in which meanings transcend their ordinary communicative functions to form a new structure in literary works. But, as I have found again, it is easier to assert than to demonstrate that process, to maintain a theory than to duplicate its tight logic in an analysis of numerous details and subtle relationships of a text.

For, as the deconstructionists have reminded us, the complexity of literary works, even the most brief, is enormous. Traditional philological study has indicated the same fact: grammar, as well as modern linguistics, demonstrating the complicated nature of language used in ordinary communication; rhetoric, as well as illocutionary theory, specifying the ways speeches are structured to effect purposes beyond simple communication; poetics, as well as literary theory, suggesting features of those texts we consider literary. It is largely with the terms of these traditional arts that I shall discuss the assumptions governing my analyses and the direction I have tried to give them.

These assumptions, as I have said, are basically structuralist in their orientation; they are derived from theorists like Roman Jakobson and Michael Riffaterre, but most particularly, from Craig La Drière. However, my main concern has not been with the iconic function of literary structures; with their deviation from standard norms; with the effect of specific genres on their development; or with overlapping systems of linguistic and literary conventions in them. Rather the focus within verbal structures has been simply on relations among different elements which are strikingly appropriate, relations which exhibit a fitness which makes structure itself a matter of interest and pleasure. For the most basic assumption here is that it is "because its internal relations are fit that a structure presents itself as unified" and thus becomes an object of aesthetic value.[9]

So while I hope to give balanced interpretations of the stories, I want also to account in some measure for their artistic achievement. My emphasis, therefore, is on their appropriately repeated and varied patterns of meaning as smaller structures are articulated in the largest divisions of the unfolding narrative; on the ways the smallest semantic elements are involved in such articulations; on the sustaining of another element which, in its context, is neither too much nor too little; on the fulfillment of expectations, as closure, completeness, and unity are achieved. To justify such emphases, three further assumptions must be discussed.

I *The first assumption is that any literary work is a speech in which meaning and effective communication are achieved by linguistic and rhetorical structuring.*

To describe any structure it is necessary to isolate the parts or elements of the structure, to describe the relations between these parts and thus to suggest the principles by which the whole is organized. In a speech, the most basic elements are the sound and meanings which operate in a particular language. These elements, especially meaning, are not always easy to analyze. But, however complex or elusive they may be, meanings are given their first shape in a speech by the grammatical rules operating in the language. Such rules (and unformulated conventions) assure that the speech will achieve the basic function of all language to establish a meaning, to communicate. The relating of words in phrases, of modifiers to modified, or subject to predicate, or clauses to sentences—all this gives a speech a grammatical structure. And what the grammatical structure of the speech produces is meaning, meaning which in any speech suggests a) a speaker; b) an addressee or audience; and, principally, c) additional objective or subjective realities, whether mountains or marriages, joys or dreams. These are the major kinds of meaning which grammarians long ago labelled in pronouns as first, second and third person meanings.

Speeches, however, are not produced simply as constructions of such meanings, but rather as purposeful instruments in life situations. Speeches are directed to goals; they are used to interest or influence others. Thus, as scattered meanings accumulate over a few paragraphs or over many pages to create a "personality" or a series of incidents to create a plot, that character may become convincing or the plot move us to compassion through a new structure of relations involving a distribution of emphases, occasional figures of speech, the deductive or inductive sequence of general and particular statements and so forth. The pressures of such directions and purposes do not destroy the grammatical structure of the speech but use it as material, so to speak, for the new structure of an *effective* communication.

A corollary, then, is that literary and non-literary speeches have grammatical and rhetorical structures similar in their purposes and functions. This simple fact has, unfortunately, been an obstacle to accurate analysis of literature. Even after several decades of text-oriented criticism, it is not unusual to find an analysis of a character in a story which parallels exactly what a biographer would say of a real person, a psychoanalyst of a patient—with attention, that is, only to the grammatical or referential structure and the rhetorical or purposive structure of the speech. There is little sense in such analysis that the literary value of the character is not in its resemblance to a real person but as part of a skillfully constructed fiction. Which is only to say that it is difficult to teach literature as literature. And that leads to a second assumption here.

Introduction

II *The second assumption here is that in a literary work, elements of grammatical and rhetorical structures are related to create an additional, an aesthetic structure.*

Any newspaper account of a crime or accident contains a predominance of narrative sentences and accumulates some minimal first and second person meanings and more extensive third person meanings. In the last instance, the accumulations of these meanings produces notions of distinguishable agents or persons, a number of actions, a time and place, and some implicit or explicit propositional notions. The following is a *New York Times* account of a theft thwarted by the police:

PARTY FOLLOWS ALLEGED PIANO THEFT

An alleged attempt to steal a piano from a Harlem school ended in a brief block party on a street nearby. The incident started in the post-midnight hours when three patrolmen saw several youths wheeling an upright piano across the intersection of Lenox Avenue and West 117th Street. The youths, spotting the patrolmen's unmarked car, fled in several directions. The patrolmen chased them into several buildings but left the piano in the middle of Lenox Avenue.

One 15-year-old was arrested. When the patrolmen returned to the piano, they found a block party had sprung up around it. Neighbors were singing and dancing, the police said, as a man played "I Left My Heart In San Francisco" on the keyboard.

More police were summoned, and the piano was wheeled away. It had apparently been stolen, the police said, from Public School 149, which is at the intersection. The 15-year-old was charged with juvenile delinquency and the police said they were searching for his alleged accomplices.

As brief as it is, the article presents a speaker, somewhat more personal and relaxed than the usual reporter of police-blotter stories; an implied, generalized, but sophisticated audience; some people involved in illegal and bizarre actions at an unusual time and place—all implying notions about the prevalence and openness of crime in the city but also suggesting some ideas about the wit and resourcefulness of city dwellers.

The paragraph could be the kernel of a short story. It would, however, undergo the mandatory transformations of fiction as such: the narrator might become omniscient; additional episodes might be created in building suspense; persons, time, and place would probably be presented in more detail; and the basic sense that nonfactual material and purposes other than truthful communication would be signaled. Together with these changes, more optional transformations influenced by prevailing conventions might occur: additional episodes might be violent or persons might reflect current television typing of police or neighborhood personalities. There would be, then, a series of changes or structuring within the larger parts of the narrative, so that a speaker becomes a "narrator," persons become "characters," a series of actions becomes a "plot," and implied propositions and smaller motifs, a "thematic structure."

But beyond such interplay of natural structure and convention (in practice, again, they are developed simultaneously) lie the more crucial decisions that create literary structure as such. Wellek and Warren, for instance, comment on brunettes and blonds in various forms of nineteenth-century literature:

Introduction

> The blond is the homemaker, unexciting but sweet. The brunette—passionate, violent, mysterious, alluring, and untrustworthy—gathers up the characteristics of the Oriental, the Jewish, the Spanish, and the Italian as seen from the point of view of the "Anglo-Saxon."[10]

But a nineteenth-century short story was not automatically a success when it had a heroine, and it was also a matter of some indifference whether she was brunette or blond. The critical decisions came after such initial choices by the writer, decisions about how she and her complex of associations were to fit into the rest of the story. But these decisions and the structures that result from them can be discussed only in the concrete instance that presents a unique set of new possibilities.

In the J. D. Salinger short story "For Esmé, With Love and Squalor," for example, it is not simply that Esmé is developed with a variety of positive and negative traits—prettiness, sensitivity, intelligence, candor, but also the awkwardness of early adolescence, insecurity, loneliness, snobbishness—and so is "well-rounded." Nor is it a matter that she can be related to certain conventional types—"the precocious little girl" that goes back at least to Carroll's Alice or to the English social type, "the proper young lady." Rather, the success of the character lies in the fact that these traits and conventional elements are developed consistently and adjusted appropriately within the norms of modern realism (with admittedly some romantic exaggeration). Esmé's unconscious fracturing of adult vocabulary is a case in point. Most instances come off in terms of humor, but the repetition of the device is not overdone. Ultimately, however, Esmé's success depends on her contrasts and balances with other characters, especially Sergeant X, with her function in the reversal of the pulp fiction convention of "the soldier's date on the last evening of the furlough," her embodiment of the basic themes of love and squalor.[11] And this process of relating is what we will see here in other cases of good characterization, in Joyce's Gabriel Conroy, Porter's María Concepción, Welty's Powerhouse.

The web of convincingly adjusted relations within and between characters can be as extensive and complex as those of Hamlet in his enormous variety and in his commerce with practically every other character in the tragedy or they can be as relatively simple as that between the dog and the mother seeking revenge (the dog mirroring her fanatical devotion and determination) in Maupassant's little story "Vendetta." Or it may be that relations are concurrently established with settings—as in the extended classic example of Hardy's *Return of the Native*—or with another part of the narrative. And such relations are more important for the literary value of the work than are questions of whether the character is realistic or fantastic, a psychological or social type, with or without allegorical significance. It may be important to recognize such conventions as they affect the intermediate parts, but it is more important to see what has been done with them in the total structure.

This is not to say that intermediate parts of a narrative, a character or plot, are not distinguishable entities or that one part may not be more successful than another. It is to say that such parts must be abstracted from a complex scattering of meanings, a bit here, a bit there.[12] If we were, then, to abstract the "traits" of Hamlet's character (as we tell students to do a character sketch) without considering his complex relations with Claudius, Gertrude, and Ophelia, we would be paraphrasing a set of grammatical and rhetorical meanings. That approach would be like describing the pearl and ignoring the black velvet which highlights it in a fine display, and does so more effectively, than would, say, Scotch plaid.[13] One wonders, then, whether the investment of time we make in having students discriminate subtle variations in types of narrators or the suspense mechanisms in a plot is not disproportionate, if it does not lead to a more holistic study of the text. It is possible, of course, that a sensitive analysis of any abstracted part can lead to its unifying intersections and interactions with other parts in the unique context of the story. But there may be more logical and more efficient ways to discover those dependencies, especially in the actual sequential sections of the whole which, very early in the history of literary analysis, Aristotle saw simply as beginning, middle, and end.

Literary quality is a property of whole works. In an important sense, it characterizes a small part of a work only in ultimate relation to the whole. In the final stages of his tribulation (to take an example again from another form), Lear reflects bitterly on the double standards of justice for rich and poor:

> Through tatter'd clothes small vices do appear,
> Robes and furr'd gowns hide all. (IV, iv, 168-169)

While there are communicative, not to say persuasive, values in this statement (the kind of insight, in fact, that a modern humanist prizes for its educational value) as well as a good use of the conventions of the proverb, the primary literary value of the sentence as a small poetic structure is its success as a set of harmonizing and contrasting patterns of sound and meaning. Ultimately, however, this value depends on the function the sentence has as a fitting part of Lear's characterization and of other patterns of meaning (the clothes motif, motifs of injustice and of sin, concealments in the plot) which were developed from the beginning of the play.

Much the same can be said for a slighter ironic phase in the opening of Salinger's "Esmé":

> Just recently, by air mail, I received an invitation to a wedding that will take place in England on April 18th. It happens to be a wedding I'd give a lot to be able to get to, and when the invitation first arrived, I thought it might just be possible for me to make the trip abroad, by plane, expenses be hanged. However, I've since discussed the matter rather extensively with my wife, a breathtakingly levelheaded girl, and we've decided against it—for one thing, I'd completely forgotten that my mother-in-law is looking forward to spending the last two weeks in April with us. I really don't get to see Mother Grencher terribly often, and she's not getting any younger. She's fifty-eight. (As she'd be the first to admit.)[14]

"My wife, a breathtakingly levelheaded girl" is clever, if also chauvinistically male. We could describe its varieties of hyperbole and irony with the tools of classical rhetoric, point to the wry humor of its context, grant it some novelty and freshness. But the tight unity and fitness of the phrase (as opposed, say, to "my spouse, a fantastically wise woman") depends on subtle adjustments of sounds and meanings: the extreme contrast of positive connotations in *breathtakingly* and the deflating of *levelheaded*; the balance of physical elements in the *breath* and *head*; the string of heavy stresses emphasizing *level*; the balance of *wife* and the deflating *girl*, as monosyllables framing the polysyllables. As interesting as such small relationships are and as important as they are for the unity and "inevitability" of the phrase, their ultimate value is their consistency with the developing characterization of the narrator-protagonist, Sergeant X, and the quite different relationships he has with his wife, other relatives, and fellow soldiers, on the one hand, and with Esmé, on the other.

But these longer structures and relationships are, in turn, developed and related within the architecture of the whole story. The most obvious feature of the total structure in the Salinger story is the division into two large parts. We can see, furthermore, that the parts are arranged symmetrically, each with a small but important introduction; a sketch of summary narration; an extended dialogue between Sergeant X and another character; and a brief postscript—with additional space setting off these sections. We could note, too, that each of the sections after the introduction has a moment of special emotion and illumination, again symmetrically placed; X's positive response to the choir, his "strongly emotional moment" of farewell, and the reprise of affectionate goodbyes, and, in the second part, his trembling reaction to the Nazi woman's inscription, his physical upset at Clay's accusation of insincerity, his healing response, finally, to Esmé's letter.

These features may support the basic division of the story and so the contrast between the love and squalor announced in the title, but they do not constitute the major unifying principle for the whole story. Something more continuous is needed, a set of meanings which, like the passage first presenting the melody of a musical composition, is thereafter repeated, varied, and contrasted in a sequence of parts which eventually becomes the complete work. It is obvious that a writer does not construct a complete plot and then return to begin his characters or his setting. Most stories begin with an account presenting most or all the elements of the narrative in a rudimentary combination in a paragraph or two or in a longer stretch. With Salinger, in the initial paragraph quoted above, we specifically get an instance of *successful* communication in a wedding invitation to the protagonist from overseas some time before April 18th. *Unsuccessful* communication is then contrasted in X's discussion with his practical wife about accepting the invitation, and more troubled communication with Mother Grencher is intimated.

In the next paragraph, there is variation, as emphasis shifts from X as protagonist to X as narrator and to his intentions in a communication to the wedding party which will become the story promised to Esmé six years before. It will presumably be a successful communication to her, perhaps momentarily unsuccessful for the groom:

> All the same, though, wherever I happen to be, I don't think I'm the type that doesn't even lift a finger to prevent a wedding from flatting. Accordingly, I've gone ahead and jotted down a few revealing notes on the bride as I knew her almost six years ago. If my notes should cause the groom, whom I haven't met, an uneasy moment or two, so much the better. Nobody's aiming to please, here. More, really, to edify, to instruct.

Thus, the beginning of the story has been put together in two paragraphs with four contrasts and variations on the initial situation. But other instances of successful or failed communication continue through the story, so that it is not too much to speak of X (or others) communicating or failing to communicate as a basic rhythm, a unifying principle of the story. In the next section, we have X's failure to communicate with other soldiers in his barracks and his lonely walk, his reaction to the choirmistress's style of talking down to the children, to the silent waitress in the tearoom, and to his stale and uncommunicative letters—a series broken, however, by his near ecstatic response to the children's singing and his first glimpse of Esmé. So the basic rhythm is not a continuous alternation of success and failure, but rather a series of one or the other, interrupted by contrasting material, with letters and conversations as instruments of the process, communion or isolation as the result.

Thus, there is a steady succession of similar and contrasting incidents which constantly draw upon the traits of evolving characters who contribute to one or other side of the process of communicating, settings which provide the proper ambience, a widening implication of themes, that is, propositional concepts, especially, about isolation and communion, love and squalor. And all of these elements proceed in the basic but complex dialectic of similarity and difference in which particular meanings are repeated, varied, contrasted as they are integrated in larger sections and parts of the story, longer series dominated by the similarity of their parts or longer systems, by their difference.[15] In this way, the unified hierarchy of the story's total structure is brought to climax and closure.

> III *The third assumption here is that a total literary structure is not simply a concatenation or a hierarchy of parts, but a system of appropriate relations within and among the parts.*

Any speech has a hierarchy of structure; so does any piece of furniture. But some tables and chairs are made so well that we feel they must be removed from their practical function (which they do not lose, of course) and be displayed in museums. Some speeches, too, are so well crafted that, without losing their communicative function, they become aesthetic objects, luminous in themselves, worthy of contemplation.

The structure of such speeches comes from the writer who has, as John Dewey says, "a grasp of the connection between what he has done and what he is to do next." As another theorist puts it, there is an

> interplay between the maker's mind and the developing structure. As relationships occur to the inventing poet in the presence of his shaping poem, he is rejecting and selecting, exploring potencies; he is reader of what has already emerged as form, or, to use Leonard Meyer's term, of "antecedents," and he himself experiences the "expectation" of the "consequents." In his choosing of this consequent rather than that, he specifies new relationships, the form is actualized more, norms are more traceable, the probability of a new particular consequent is increased.[16]

The structuring of the literary work is, thus, a progressive work in which certain possibilities arise once the writer begins, and, then, are appropriately selected and combined, are capitalized upon as new relationships within parts and between parts in the sequence of the story are made. For Salinger, this was a matter of avoiding sentimentality in the long conversation of Esmé and Sergeant X or modulating the relatively tolerant irony of X in the first part to the sarcastic tone appropriate to his nervous condition and the obtuseness of Clay, in the second.

But these are only two of numerous problems of sustaining one meaning with consistency (and yet surprise) or modulating to a contrast with another meaning in the sequence of parts. Similar choices have to be made "laterally" within each part, as the action, thought, and speech of characters are related to the materials of setting or the thematic implications. At every juncture, as the right word, connotation, or sound is found for the right place, the relations created radiate that fitness which is the essential achievement of art. When what ought to be done is done, a system of relations is built which dominates any meaning or convention which it involves, a sense of structure simply as structure, enjoyable in itself.

My effort in the following analyses, to repeat, is to provide an interpretation of various stories with due attention to current scholarship about them. But it is, also, to trace, at some points, this literary structure in the stories. Thus, I have tried to show that whether Gabriel Conroy is redeemed at the end of "The Dead" is a problem of interpretation but may be less important for explaining the story's success than how a network of functional and personal relationships is fitly developed; that the basic rhythm of secrets in Lawrence's "Rocking-Horse Winner" is the successful mediating device for flat characterizations and symbols of the story; that the literary structure of O'Connor's "Artificial Nigger" centrally involves the similarities and differences of the two main characters. These are not structures that we necessarily are conscious of as we first encounter a story. But they are features that we seem to respond to as we read and enjoy the story—and that we make clearer to ourselves in analysis.

But the closer the work approaches to the fit structure demanded by its own logic, the more difficult it is to assess or demonstrate its achievement. Mistakes, failures to meet a demand the work has obviously generated for itself, are usually easier to detect. What one does, though, to assess positive value is to gather support for the initial impression that fit relation does exist by showing that structure itself does exist where at first it might not have seemed to; by contrasting or comparing to grasp better what the uniqueness of the structure is; by checking one's impression with that of others. In such work conclusive demonstration is not possible, of course. But progress is, even though one returns to the impression one had to begin with. For critical analysis is not circular. Rather it is spiral, in deepening knowledge of the text: it strengthens or weakens, perhaps displaces one's first impression; it leads to corroboration by others that what ought to be, is, that the literary structure itself, the harmonious dance of the elements together, is the value we are responding to, so that nothing more, nothing less, nothing rearranged will do.[17]

Notes

[1] For convenient collections of theories about the short story, see Hollis Summers ed., *Discussions of the Short Story* (Boston: D. C. Heath & Co., 1963); Charles E. May ed., *Short Story Theories* (Athens: Ohio University Press, 1976); and Susan Lohafer and Jo Ellyn Clarey eds., *Short Story Theory at a Crossroads* (Baton Rouge: Louisiana State University Press, 1989).

[2] See, for example, Norman Friedman, "What Makes a Short Story Short?" *Modern Fiction Studies* 4 (Summer, 1958): 103-17, and Theodore A. Stroud, "A Critical Approach to the Short Story," *The Journal of General Education* 9 (January, 1956): 91-100; both of these essays are reprinted in May.

[3] See, however, Mary Rohrberger and Dan E. Burns, "Short Fiction and the Numinous Realm: Another Attempt at Definition," *Modern Fiction Studies* 28 (Spring, 1982): 5-12, and the perceptive discussion by Mary Louis Pratt, "The Short Story: the Long and Short of It," *Poetics* 10 (June, 1981): 175-193, in which she argues for a generic dependence of the short story on the novel and in the shorter form distinguishes between what can be called universal or constitutive factors (e.g., "short," "prose," "fiction") and regulative factors, widespread tenden-

cies like the "incomplete or fragmentary" quality of many short stories. For a variety of approaches to genre theory as such, see other essays in *Poetics 10*, especially Marie-Loure Ryan, "On the Why, What and How of Generic Taxonomy"; J. Craig La Drière, "Classification," in *Dictionary of World Literary Terms*, ed. Joseph T. Shipley (Boston: The Writer, Inc., 1970); Paul Hernadi, *Beyond Genre: New Directions in Literary Classification* (Ithaca: Cornell University Press, 1972); Joseph P. Strelka ed., *Theories of Literary Genre* (University Park: The Pennsylvania State University Press, 1978); Alastair Fowler, *Kinds of Literature* (Cambridge: Harvard University Press, 1983.)

[4]But see Suzanne C. Ferguson, "Defining the Short Story: Impressionism and Form," *Modern Fiction Studies* 28 (Spring, 1982): 13-24.

[5]Edgar Allan Poe, "Review of Twice-Told Tales," in May, 48.

[6]See La Drière, "Scientific Method in Criticism," in *Dictionary of World Literary Terms*.

[7]While I have little sympathy with the recent attacks on the most basic assumptions of interpretation, I recognize that the performance of modern interpreters is not always brilliant. In reviewing the literature on the stories dealt with here, I was surprised, for example, at how often matters of "fact"—when X received the letter or Y lost the package—were reported inaccurately (though doubtless someone will find similar inaccuracies here). Simply to describe something accurately *is* a difficult job. More subjectively, I felt that some interpretations give too much or too little weight to one or another element in the text; that literal meaning is neglected in the pursuit of implication; that establishing an unnecessarily detailed faithfulness to a mythic or Biblical analogue is the overriding concern; that a story is discussed mainly in terms of its role in a collection (whether *Dubliners* or *Go Down, Moses*) or the larger context of an author's whole work, its thematic elements as part of his philosophy. Too often, that is, the text is being considered not on its own merits but in relation to something else. On the other

hand, unusual insights about the stories are not infrequent, and there is often an intuitive sense of what is aesthetically important. Above all, there is usually a broad consensus about the general meaning of a text, and that is what I have tried to reflect here. My debts, then, are certainly larger than my reservations.

[8] Susan Sontag, *Against Interpretation* (New York: Dell Publishing, 1966), 12-13.

[9] J. Craig La Drière, "Fitness," in *Dictionary of World Literary Terms*.

[10] René Wellek and Austin Warren, *Theory of Literature* (New York: Harcourt, Brace, 1949), 228.

[11] For a fuller analysis, see Daniel Burke, FSC, "Salinger's Esmé: Some Matters of Balance," *Modern Fiction Studies* 12 (1966): 341-47.

[12] In recent years, analysis of the natural parts of narrative and the conventions of their presentation has been pursued in great detail. For surveys of this material, see Seymour Chatman, *Story and Discourse* (Ithaca: Cornell University Press, 1980); Shlomith Rimmon-Kenan, *Narrative Fiction: Contemporary Poetics* (London: Methuen, 1983); Tzvetan Todorov, *The Poetics of Prose* (Oxford: Blackwell, 1977); and, among earlier studies, Wayne Booth, *The Rhetoric of Fiction* (Chicago: University of Chicago Press, 1961). For application of such material to the short story, see Susan Lohafer, *Coming to Terms With the Short Story* (Baton Rouge: Louisiana State University Press, 1983).

[13] The emphasis here on aesthetic pattern is, it might seem, as much a rejection of the value of referential meaning as that of the deconstructionists. Not so. These values—simply descriptive of reality or more complexly humanistic and ethical—are part of the grammatical and rhetorical structures which the literary speech retains even as they provide material for its aesthetic structure. Such a view implies that aesthetic response is usually mixed, dominantly to the structure of fit

relations but with awareness of the natural structures and response to them. The situation is not unlike that of physical vision: focusing on one part of an object does not blind us to other parts, though they are less in focus, nor prevent us from focusing on those parts, if we choose. The critical problem is to discriminate the aesthetic from other elements of our response and to relate it to specific features of the text. On mixed response see William J. Rooney, *The Problem of Poetry and Belief in Contemporary Criticism*, (Washington: Catholic University Press, 1949), 115-18.

[14] J.D. Salinger, *Nine Stories* (Boston: Little, Brown, and Co., 1953), 91.

[15] "Serial organization is the order of recurrence of some identity; such organization operates to *diffuse* an established identity: it is exemplified typically by metrical rhythm. Systematic organization, on the other hand, operates to establish new identities by *concentration*, or cumulation, of elements into relatively discrete unitary entities. To take an example from rhythmic structure, the foot is a small system; the strophe a larger system. The normal interaction of the two types of organization is illustrated in these examples. You must have some systematic unit, which may be repeated, before you can have a series; you must have a foot if you are to have a meter. But you can constitute a larger system serially, simply by "marking off" a certain number of repetitions of the smaller system: so lines and stanzas may be constructed, by serial organization of small units (feet) into cumulative systems of a larger order; and then these larger systems in turn may be repeated serially again, or ordered into yet larger systems. The interaction, or interinvolvement of the two types of order occurs at all levels and tends always to be complementary," La Drière, "Literary Form and Form in the Other Arts," in *Stil und Form Probleme in der Literatur*, ed. Paul Bockman (Heidelberg: Winter, 1959): 34.

[16] Sr. Mary Francis Slattery, "Formal Specification," *Journal of Aesthetics and Art Criticism* 25 (1966): 86.

[17] Material in the Introduction here has been adapted from my *Notes on Literary Structure* (Washington: University Press of America, 1982).

James Joyce: Gabriel and the Women of "The Dead"

Joyce's densely textured story of a holiday party in Dublin follows its protagonist, Gabriel Conroy, through two stages that evening. The first stage is dominated by a number of frustrations before he gives his successful after-dinner speech; the second mounts through rather happy moments to a climactic reversal, as his wife Gretta tells of an earlier love in her life. Within a larger web of relationships and sometimes oppressive concerns about failure that counterpoint the festivity of the occasion, both series focus on Gabriel's interactions with women. With his three hostesses, these interactions are largely in functional roles, with Lily, Molly and Gretta, in more personal roles. And in a basic pattern of the story, the incidents are alternated with his reactions to them and his reflections about them. As the themes of the story are gradually deepened and complicated by Gabriel's reflections, the direct statements of his speech and conversation at the dinner, and the

> *accumulated implication of symbols and patterns of connotations, he is brought to a less selfish understanding of his own humanity and, in his final meditation and the lyric conclusion, to an appreciation of the individuality of others and their bonds with him in the common mortality of all.*

"The Dead" is the crowning achievement of Joyce's *Dubliners* and, perhaps, the century's most nearly perfect short story. One is understandably intimidated by this perfection and by the complexities which Joyce has reduced to such brilliant unity. Any new analysis of the story may seem, in fact, pointless or at least belated. But a classic never yields all of its secrets; its success is a continuing challenge to seek them.

As critics have been observing for several decades now, the search is complicated because "The Dead" develops several different kinds of meaning in extraordinarily convincing fashion.[1] The story is a report of a rather petty society, though not without its saving graces; it is a suggestive portrait of one troubled Dubliner, Gabriel Conroy, who grows significantly in the course of one evening; it is a profound and moving reflection on the dark shadow which mortality casts over the superficial encounters and the deeper bonds of humanity. And most simply, it is a description of a Christmas holiday party that three musically talented spinsters are giving, as they have for many years, for their relatives and friends, two of whom stay over in the city that evening. But the deeper resonances of these meanings and their subtle interactions, their steady progress to more complex emotions and insights, their ascent finally to the lyric conclusion—these are the mysteries of the story's success.

If we begin with the largest temporal divisions of the narrative, we see that the activities of the festive evening provide the basic framework of "The Dead"; they fall roughly into six stages, the natural stages of such an evening.[2] The opening part recounts the arrivals at the party, particularly of Gabriel and his wife Gretta, and the initial mingling of the guests; the second describes several dances and musical presentations, concluding with Aunt Julia's song; the third presents the supper, its lively conversation, and Gabriel's speech of thanks to the hostesses; the fourth includes the departures of guests and Gabriel and Gretta's walk and cab ride to the hotel where they had decided to stay overnight; the fifth is the major climax as Gabriel's desire for his wife is thwarted by her distressed revelation of an innocent earlier love; the sixth is denouement, with Gabriel's drowsy thoughts on love and mortality that shade off into a symbolic description of a snowfall which poetically transfigures these and other themes.

The first paragraph of the story presents two kinds of involvements in the activities of the evening. First, there is Lily, "literally run off her feet," assisting the male guests as they arrive. Her involvement could be called *functional*, a service or conventional social behavior that is impersonal or perfunctory, perhaps concerned with coping satisfactorily, but also open to making a good impression or achieving some selfish advantage. On the other hand, there is the involvement of the hostesses "gossiping and laughing and fussing" as they welcome the guests. Their involvement is more *personal*, concerned primarily with human relationships, enjoying the interaction of friends and festivity.

The difference of styles is not absolute, of course, it is a matter of emphasis and proper balance. As we soon learn, Lily has some slight social ties with at least one of the guests and a cordial, though recently troubled, relationship with her employers. And Aunt Kate and Julia do fuss over practical concerns for the success of the party.

But involvements in the activities of the party, with one or other of these emphases, constitutes the basic building block of the story's structure. The next two paragraphs begin the repetition, variation, and contrast of its elements with a brief account of functional arrangements or duties in the household but also its comfortable provisioning, and, then, some specific functional concerns for the party's success that evening.

Together, then, these two paragraphs serve as an introduction to Gabriel Conroy. As protagonist, he is very much at the center of the evening's activities in *functional* roles: participating in the conversations, joining in the dancing and dining, responding to the musical presentations, and, even more, discharging the duties he has been given by his aunts as overseer of the tipsy Freddy Malins, as carver of the goose, and as after-dinner speaker. In these activities, Gabriel is rooted in the naturalistically detailed narrative, and, as he usually succeeds in these functions, the increments to his characterization are positive. On the other hand, in his *personal* roles as nephew, friend, citizen, or husband (the last, of course, becoming primary), he is less successful and the negative side of his characterization expands more significantly in these directions. This latter development occurs in a series of faux pas but, then, in Gabriel's reflections about the situations. It is especially in this self-consciousness, so often with bruising uncertainty and self-deprecation—and in moments of withdrawal from the busy proceedings at hand—that we are led to more wide and fundamental issues about Gabriel's social group, his country, his basic humanity. And it is in the aftermath of the party, as the focus is narrowed to Gabriel and Gretta and then to Gabriel alone, that frustrated passion yields to deeper reflection which, in turn, crystallizes brilliantly in the conclusion.

But, once again, the story unfolds most directly as a sequence of successful or flawed involvements in the party. In the first section, for example, after the introductory paragraphs, we see Gabriel confuse functional and social relationships with Lily and, then, withdraw to worry over his mistake and his approaching duties as after-dinner speaker; reveal himself in the teasing thrusts of his wife and aunts as an overprotective father and husband; be compared, by implication, with the earthy and witty Mr. Browne, who also mistakes his audience, and, then, with the tipsy and voluble Freddy Malins.

What an outline of incidents does not suggest, of course, is the scope and fullness of the story. In part, this unusually concentrated significance results from the variety of characters and their interactions, in part, from the crowded sequence of scenes, each of which, however, is distinctly realized and dramatically structured—all comfortably accommodated within the ample length of the short story. A profusion of precise, realistic detail also contributes to this concentration, as in the description of the buffet (196-197).[3]

But more important for the meaningfulness of the story is the use of such complete descriptive naturalism in the development of other structures, particularly in the gradual widening and deepening of thematic implication. In the rather Dickensian description of the buffet, for instance, the military imagery ("Between these rival ends ran parallel lines . . . sentries . . . a pudding . . . lay in waiting . . . three squads of bottles . . . drawn up according to the colours of their uniform . . . smallest squad . . . transverse green sashes") prepares most immediately for Gabriel's remarks in the same facetious vein that "we have been recipients—or perhaps, I had better say, the victims—of the hospitality of certain good ladies" (202). But the imagery also relates to Gabriel's fear of being victimized socially and to the wider and ironic notion of heroism in the story: military glory and its passion, as recalled in the statues of heroes and patriots, are beyond the limited aspiration of this society and especially of Gabriel Conroy. There is further irony in Gabriel's encounter with Molly Ivors in a dance called *lancers* and, more generally a *quadrille* (from the display exercise of French knights with their horses) and that his view of himself in the hotel room is from a *cheval* mirror. More crucially, Gretta's revelation at the climax precipitates in Gabriel "a vague terror . . . as if in that hour when he had hoped to triumph some impalpable and vindictive being was coming against him, gathering forces against him in its vague world" (220).

Of course, it is now a commonplace that in *Dubliners* Joyce follows "Flaubert in making every detail of description and dialogue part of both a 'mood' and a highly developed symbolic pattern."[4] Thus, the close texture of recurrent imagery has provided an exciting, if not always a happy, hunting ground for the analyst in search of the one symbol which dominates and pulls the whole structure together. Perhaps the most that should be said, however, is that in "The Dead" a particularly strong contrast evolves between the realistically detailed but rather ordinary activities of the celebration and the often ambiguous suggestiveness and weightiness of the concurrent symbolism. Among the stories of *Dubliners*, this contrast is unusual here in degree rather than in kind, but it is important in the total structure of "The Dead." And Joyce's success in maintaining its density, evolving it so consistently and in such detail, and finally resolving it in the lyric apotheosis of several key images at the conclusion—is an achievement that contributes much to the story's aesthetic value.

Gabriel's psychodrama is, also, set in a larger network of relationships sketched among the characters, with special emphasis, again, on their roles and duties and with precise detailing in their presentation. The opening sentence of the story is a paradigm of these and several other elements: "Lily, the caretaker's daughter, was literally run off her feet." As we enter the scene of the party already begun, we see the housemaid about her assigned duty of answering the door and assisting the guests as they arrive. There are so many guests in a short time, however, that she is said to be just coping with the job. She seems threatened with failure, the first of many threatened failures in the story.

She is also identified immediately in terms of a family relationship and a social class. But there is a quick switch involved here, from the heightened associations of her name (with death, as the conventional flower of funerals, and with resurrection, as the flower of Easter, as also with poetry, Pre-Raphaelite preciocity, the Virgin, the Archangel Gabriel in depictions of the Annunciation) to her working-class father and his job. There are numerous small contrasts of this type in the story, usually between middle class pretension and the provincial reality of Dublin, as in the next sentence between "gentlemen" and "the little pantry behind the office." These small verbal structures are quietly accumulated to become an important part of central themes in "The Dead" and in the *Dubliners* as a whole—*paralysis*, the inability of characters to act significantly; *gnomon*, their hampered growth and incompleteness as individuals.[6]

After describing more of Lily's duties, which significantly have the Irish female serving the male, the first paragraph goes on to mention not simply the arrival of guests but also Lily's relationships to her employers. She does not have to attend to the ladies. Kate and Julia have this function, as well as the problem of thinking out arrangements for a "dressing room" (contrast with bathroom). But they greet the ladies in an amicable and relaxed fashion, "gossiping and laughing and fussing." As they peer over the bannister and call down to Lily, we are given a picture of the put-upon servant downstairs and the fussy, if not unkindly, employers upstairs—and the difficult communication between them.[5] Moreover, as with the separate reception of the male and female guests at the beginning, it is emphasized that the dark staircase is a locus and symbolic instrument of such separations.

In the second and third paragraphs of the story, the narrator continues in a chatty fashion, the voice not of an impersonal and distant omniscience but rather of a close and knowledgeable friend of the family. But now the mood is reflective and the purpose historical, as he steps away from the scene to establish, with proper Irish hyperbole, the continuous success of the affair. He then provides background for the generous hospitality of Kate, Julia, and Mary Jane; their numerous relationships with others and their mutual support among themselves; the duties of their modest life and their enjoyment of good food; and, again, their relations with Lily; and their concerns for the evening. In the process, norms are introduced for what dominantly successful human relationships are.

But the relationships are not simply among the living. As the history of the festivity is reviewed (and the long perspective may imply that many of the principals are no longer alive at the time of the narration itself), it is specified that the tradition began after Pat Morkan's death thirty years ago, when his sisters moved to the "dark, gaunt house on Usher's Island." From this initial reference to a death and the change that followed it, relationships with the dead as those to be remembered, admired, scorned, annoyed at, honored or feared will ramify to the end of the story. And only at the end will relations between the living and the dead achieve coherence.[7]

Thus, most appropriately for the larger structuring of the story, the opening develops essential background for the activities and reflections of the hero (whose entrance, therefore, has been delayed)—the contrast between success and failure and, more specifically, the tension between carefree festivity and worried concern, or social accommodation and social pretension, or, most important, successful and unsuccessful human relationships. The drama of success and failure is then narrowed down to Gabriel's activities this evening and his reflections about them, to his roles here and in life generally, to his discharge of his responsibilities and his desire to escape from them. In the process, the repeated shift from incident to reflection constitutes an accompanying structural pattern in the story.[8]

The swing from external situation into Gabriel's consciousness occurs especially in his three major contretemps. The first of these, with Lily the caretaker's daughter, is presented even before the physical description of Gabriel. Preparation for their exchange, however, includes notes that he is the guest most expected, feels put upon as the conventional husband-in-waiting ("they forget that my wife here takes three mortal hours to dress herself"); appears cheerfully dutiful to his aunts; is much protected against the snow; is meticulous about his appearance; is snobbish about Lily's mispronunciation; is playing the social role of older family friend with the servant girl.

—Tell me Lily, he said in a friendly tone, do you still go to school?

—O no, sir, she answered. I'm done schooling this year and more.

> —O, then, said Gabriel gayly, I suppose we'll be going to your wedding one of these fine days with your young man, eh?
>
> The girl glanced back at him over her shoulder and said with great bitterness:
>
> —The men that is now is only all palaver and what they can get out of you. (178)

As in the later incidents, the response Gabriel expects is completely reversed. He thus misjudges a situation, fumbles in dealing with it, and is put on the defensive by the woman involved. Given Gabriel's relationship to Lily, this is the least important of the three incidents—and properly so, of course, since the buildup to the encounter with Gretta is a major progression in the narrative. But the exchange does posit important issues: the condition of Irish manhood and the proper relation of man and woman.

These are issues that Gabriel is not yet ready to face. So he blushes, fusses with his clothing, and compounds his mistake with a patronizing tip to Lily. And he withdraws as quickly as possible to his troubled reflections:

> He waited outside the drawing-room door until the waltz should finish, listening to the skirts that swept against it and the shuffling of feet. He was still discomposed by the girl's bitter and sudden retort. It had cast a gloom over him which he tried to dispel by arranging his cuffs and the bows of his tie. Then he took from his waistcoat pocket a little paper and glanced at the headings he had made for his speech. He was undecided about the lines from Robert Browning for he

feared they would be above the heads of his hearers. Some quotation that they could recognize from Shakespeare or from the Melodies would be better. The indelicate clacking of the men's heels and the shuffling of their soles reminded him that their grade of culture differed from his. He would only make himself ridiculous by quoting poetry to them which they could not understand. They would think that he was airing his superior education. He would fail them just as he had failed with the girl in the pantry. He had taken up a wrong tone. His whole speech was a mistake from first to last, an utter failure. (179)

Defensiveness, snobbery, an almost paranoid anxiety about his speech and its possible effects on the other guests—these are some of the negatives we see in Gabriel and see him exaggerating in several instances. A more balanced perspective is available to us, however, as we see Gabriel in his various public functions re-establishing his self-confidence to some extent before the more complicated and abrasive encounter with Miss Ivors. And as the characterization evolves, there are inputs from his memories of the past (he is proud of his mother's intelligence, but angered by her attitude to Gretta) and by a series of implicit and explicit contrasts with other characters.

It can be said briefly that in these contrasts Gabriel comes off better with the men than with the women, with Freddy Malins, Mr. Browne, Mr. D'Arcy, or the nameless men, than with his aunts and Jane—and more particularly with Molly Ivors and Gretta. For all their fussiness, the "Three Graces" have a simplicity and generosity in the hospitality which Joyce celebrates here which contrasts with the formal sociability and self-concern of Gabriel. And with Miss Ivors and Gretta there are presented a womanly freedom, a directness (the words *frankly* and *frank-mannered* occur in *Dubliners* only with the women of "The Dead"), a lack of sophistication identified with the west of Ireland and its past and more passionate commitments that, in turn, are foils to Gabriel's continental pretensions, his social role-playing, and his mediocrities. For all this difference, and for all the difference which Gabriel sees between himself and his fellow Dubliners generally, there is a common ground on which he meets them. And indeed the paralysis of Dublin's living-dead as well as its "ingenuous insularity" are part of that ground, though not the major part.

As Gabriel's characterization is developed, therefore, we see an ambiguous mix of admirable and unfortunate traits. We see that he is limited in his aspiration; he is neither the man who will leave his country, though he says he is sick of it, nor the man who will die for love of it—or of a woman. He does not have a proper esteem for himself and, almost as a direct result, he is not humanly in touch with those around him. "What did he care that his aunts were only two ignorant old women," he thinks, and he asks of Miss Ivors whether that "girl or woman, or whatever she was . . . had . . . really any life of her own behind all of her propagandism." What Gabriel does not perceive in any depth is the life behind the everyday presence of friends, relatives, even Gretta and Ireland itself. It is only after the deep wounding of his pride by Molly Ivors and, more especially, Gretta's unconscious destruction of his image as the protective and masterful husband that he appears to be accepting of himself, of Gretta in her deeper reality—and thence of the deepest bonds of all men in their aspiration and their common mortality.

While it is possible to speak of a direct and steady rise in the narrative to the climactic hotel room scenes, it seems, more specifically, that Gabriel's progress to enlightenment goes through the cycles suggested there. In the first cycle, there is a steady decline for Gabriel into frustration, not simply through the major exchanges with Lily and Molly Ivors but even in his teasing session with Gretta and his aunts ("Gabriel knitted his brows and said, as if he were slightly angered . . . "[181]) and in his brief but sharp exchange with Gretta about vacationing in the west of Ireland ("You can go if you like, said Gabriel coldly," and Gretta, "There's a nice husband for you, Mrs. Malins" [191]). Even old Mrs. Malins, with whom Gabriel seeks refuge from Molly, insists on talking about the sea captain who was attentive to her and the son-in-law who on vacation trips is, by implied contrast with Gabriel, obliging and unselfish. There is momentary relief for Gabriel from this dominant trend, in his functional roles and in the unexpected but pure escape as he listens to Aunt Julia's song (even beyond his imagined escapes to the snowy outdoors). But the cycle is finally ended and clearly reversed only by Gabriel's speech, nervously begun, then warmly received as it rather strikingly achieves its rhetorical goals for the occasion.

In the sung toast to the hostesses after his speech, however, stress is laid on the words "Unless he tell a lie." And the speech, from another point of view, does ring hollow. For while Gabriel addresses himself to noble sentiments, indeed to thematic issues of basic importance in the story, his conventional phrasing shows him to be without deep personal understanding or commitment. The dramatic irony is clear (especially in his barb for the absent Molly Ivors) that he had still to learn about proper self-regard ("my poor powers as a speaker"); the tradition of "genuine warm-hearted courteous Irish hospitality"; the qualities "of humanity . . . of kindly humor"; the right balance of reverence for "the dead and gone great ones" and concern for "living duties and living affections." It will be Gretta's role to demonstrate how she embodies these qualities so strikingly that Gabriel can see her and then his aunts and others in a totally new light.

The second cycle begins after the speech and toast and moves in a quite different manner. It takes Gabriel from his success at the dinner table through a mounting series of pleasantly emotional moments: his successful but somewhat unkind story telling at the expense of grandfather Morkan; the hilarity of the confused leave-takings; the quiet reaction to Gretta as she stands listening to distant music, and the picture he makes of the scene; the pleasure of the walk and his tender memories of Gretta; his erotic expectation; Gretta's kiss. To these dominants, there is a subordinate contrast of delay, Gretta's abstraction, or the digression about Freddy Malin's repayment of a debt. But the cycle ends with an even more resounding reversal with Gretta's tearful breakdown. The revelations about Michael Furey then lead Gabriel step by step from anger and frustration to sympathy and understanding in a dramatically brilliant scene that has received detailed attention from the commentators.

It should be noted further that both these cycles are pitched at a rather high level of intensity and emphasis—and that they reach still higher levels not only in the inherent excitement of their conclusions but also in the less perceptible cumulation of some key semantic elements. The first cycle, especially, involves not only a long series of *anticipations* and *anxieties* related mainly to the party but also a frequent *intensity* and *dynamism* in the diction ("run off her feet . . . clanged . . . scamper . . . scraping vigorously . . . high color of his cheeks pushed upward"—to take only a few examples at the opening) and, as indicated before, the exaggerations of colloquial Irish speech ("a great affair . . . everybody came . . . never once . . . splendid style . . . not wish for worlds . . . dreadfully afraid . . . must be perished alive"). But again there are subordinate contrasts with the frequent element of *limitation*: in simple collocations ("old as they were—her aunts also did their share; Julia—though she was quite grey; though their life was modest—they believed in eating well") or in the literal but very relative distinction of middle-class achievement ("she had the organ in Haddington Road. Many of her pupils belonged to better-class families . . . still the leading soprano in Adam and Eve's"). And to such prosaic limitations, often enough sensibly dealt with by the women, relate the grander frustrations of Gabriel, the larger themes of Dublin's paralysis, and the theme of mortality itself.

The second cycle retains some of these elements (especially the "scattering" and "helter-skelter" sememes of the dynamism group) but is further characterized by impetuous *wave* imagery ("A sudden tide of joy went leaping out of his heart . . . the blood went bounding in his veins . . . a wave of yet more tender joy escaped from his heart and went coursing in warm flood along his arteries") and elements of *tenderness* and *lightness* ("no word tender enough . . . call her softly . . . she leaned lightly . . . feet falling in soft thuds . . . lightly on his shoulders . . . . He was very delicate"). The contrastive and subordinate elements here are in the *military* images noted earlier and continued here to the climax ("Now that she had fallen to him" and, again, "some impalpable and vindictive being was coming against him, gathering forces against him in its vague world") and strengthened by additional images of *pressure* and *violence* ("catch her by the shoulders . . . pressed her arm . . . flung his arms . . . to seize her and only the stress of his nails . . . to take her as she was would be brutal . . . to master her strange mood . . . to crush her body against his, to overmaster her"). One of the significant achievements of the story, therefore, is how it moves from a high level of contrasting strain and liveliness to much higher levels of intense emotion at the climax without undue effort or solemnity (most of the *laughter*, especially the *hearty* laughter of the *Dubliners* is in "The Dead"). And this particular success relates to the control of imagistic and other semantic recurrences noted here.

One tends to agree with Kenneth Burke and many other commentators that the structure of "The Dead" is peculiarly oriented to Gabriel's vision of the falling snow and that in this conclusion the evolving concerns, expectations, and patterns of the story reach their completion in a remarkable fashion. As Gabriel reaches a new level of understanding in his lengthy meditation in the denouement, breaks out of his undue self-concern, and becomes capable of a deeper relationship with Gretta, his aunts, and others, the snow becomes, in Burke's terms, a symbol of "transcendence above the conditioned." It falls upon the living and the dead who are merged in the commonality of human aspiration unmarked by divisiveness, as in the love of Gabriel and Michael for Gretta. The snow, too, "general all over Ireland," covers the division of country-west ("the primitive, untutored, impulsive country from which Gabriel had felt himself alienated")[9] and city-east, a unity Gabriel suggests that he, too, may achieve in his "journey westward." And in the vision of the snowfall, many other motifs find a new unity: mastery and military valor ("snow was general . . . mutinous waves . . . spears of the little gate"), light and dark, withdrawal and imagined scene, softness and tenderness, warped religion and true redemption—and, above all, the theme of mortality itself. With Beck I would emphasize that the "snow falling faintly through the universe" is an abstraction that has emerged "out of particular realities."[10] Much the same can be said for the more restricted symbols which come together in the comprehensive and intense concentration to the final paragraph and achieve a deeply satisfying sense of completion.[11]

Our concern here has been to probe some of the major structures and narrative rhythms of "The Dead" and to suggest that Joyce has developed them with unusual consistency and fitness. The basic rhythm of successful and flawed involvements in the activities of the party; the ironic patterning of Gabriel's involvements in two cycles—through frustrations to success in his practical duties and, thereafter, through emotional satisfactions to his climactic frustrations and epiphany; the well-managed alternation of scene and reflection; the general contrast of detailed realism and rich symbolism evolving, with consistent control of connotation and implication, to the snow vision—all contribute significantly to the magnificent coherence of the story.

Notes

[1] Among earlier analyses of the story which are particularly interesting are Warren Beck, *Joyce's Dubliners: Substance, Vision and Art* (Durham, N.C.: Duke University Press, 1969), 303-60; Samuel N. Bogorad, "Gabriel Conroy as 'White Sepulchre,'" *Forum* (Ball State) 14:i (1973): 52-148; J.D. Boyd and R.A. Boyd, "The Love Triangle in Joyce's 'The Dead,'" *University of Toronto Quarterly* 42 (1973): 202-17; Homer O. Brown, *James Joyce's Early Fiction* (Cleveland: Press of Case-Western Reserve University, 1972), 85-103; Kenneth Burke, "Three Definitions," *Kenyon Review* 13 (1951): 186-92; David Daiches, *The Novel and the Modern World* (Chicago, University of Chicago Press, 1939), 91-100; Paul Deane, "Motion Picture Techniques in James Joyce's 'The Dead,'" *James Joyce Quarterly* 6 (1969): 231-36; Richard Ellmann, *James Joyce* (New York: Oxford University Press, 1959), 252-63; John W. Foster, "Passage through 'The Dead,'" *Criticism* 15 (1973): 91-108;

Hugh Kenner, *Dublin's Joyce* (Bloomington: Indiana University Press, 1956), 62-68; Richard Levin and Charles Shattuck, "First Flight to Ithaca: A New Reading of Joyce's 'Dubliners,'" in *James Joyce: Two Decades of Criticism*, ed. Seon Givens (New York: Vanguard Press, 1948), 87-92; Marvin Magalaner and Richard M. Kain, *Joyce: The Man, the Work, the Reputation* (New York: New York University Press, 1956), 92-98; Arthur McGuinness, "The Ambience of Space in Joyce's 'The Dead,'" *Studies in Short Fiction* 11 (1974): 343-51; Frank O'Connor, "Joyce and Disassociated Metaphor," in *The Mirror in The Roadway: A Study of the Modern Novel* (New York: Knopf, 1956), 299-301; Brendan P. O'Hehir, "Structural Symbol in Joyce's 'The Dead,'" *Twentieth Century Literature* 3 (April, 1957): 3-13; Epifano San Juan, Jr., *James Joyce and the Craft of Fiction* (Rutherford, N.J.: Fairleigh Dickinson University Press, 1972), 209-33; Allen Tate, "Three Commentaries," *Sewanee Review* 58 (Winter, 1950): 15-25; William York Tindall, *The Literary Symbol* (New York: Columbia University Press, 1955), 224-28; and Florence Walzl, "Gabriel and Michael: The Conclusion of 'The Dead,'" *James Joyce Quarterly* 4 (1966): 17-31. It will be evident to anyone even slightly familiar with scholarship on "The Dead" that several of the alternatives which critics have developed and argued over the years have been consciously adopted here. This analysis assumes, for instance, that, despite his manifest limitations, Gabriel is not irrevocably one of Dublin's living-dead and that his experience at the conclusion is basically redemptive.

[2]See Burke, 186, who sees three divisions (beginning of the party, the party at its height, the events following the party) and Beck, 313, who sees two main sections (the party and the scene at the hotel). The sections discussed here are, of course, smaller units in Burke's divisions, each with several events contrasted with Gabriel's reactions and reflections. But Joyce has complicated any sense of successive parts by intertwining characters and themes rather tightly in the progressive

stages of the evening, while at the same time separating three sections with leaders, the final scene with additional space.

[3] Page references in parentheses are to *Dubliners*, a corrected text by Robert Scholes, in consultation with Richard Ellmann (New York: The Viking Press, 1968); the military imagery in this passage has been noted recently by, among others, Terence Brown, "The Dublin of *Dubliners*," in Suheil Bushrui and Bernard Benstock, eds., *James Joyce: An International Perspective* (Totowa, N.J. : Barnes and Noble, 1982), 16. The imagery has been traced through the entire subtext of the story by Adrienne Auslander Munich, "Form and Subtext in Joyce's 'The Dead,'" *Modern Philology* 82 (November, 1986): 173-84.

[4] A. Walton Litz and Robert Scholes, eds., *Dubliners: Text, Criticism, and Notes* (New York: Viking, 1969), 298.

[5] Unsatisfactory communication in "The Dead" is discussed by Winston Weathers, *The Broken Word: The Communication Pathos in Modern Literature* (New York: Gordon and Breach, 1981), 125-27, and, in terms of "noise" affecting communication, by Ross Chambers, *Story and Situation: Narrative Seduction and the Power of Fiction* (Minneapolis: University of Minnesota Press, 1984), 181-204.

[6] On Lily, see Tilly Eggers, "What Is a Woman . . . a Symbol of?" *James Joyce Quarterly* 18 (Summer, 1981): 382-83.

[7] Ellmann speaks magisterially about the role of the dead in the story, which after all, bears their name as title (2nd edition, 243-53). "It is one of Joyce's achievements as fictionist that throughout *Dubliners* almost every figure, however slight the role, can loom as a possible protagonist in another story. The potential becomes strong in an intermediate character such as Mary Jane, who not only transcends Gabriel's conventional description in his speech as 'talented, cheerful, hard-working, and the best of nieces,' but is also recognizable for much beyond what the story specifies" (Beck, 325). Beck's analysis (Beck,

321-29) of Mary Jane's role in the story that leads to this conclusion is detailed and convincing.

[8] For a detailed analysis of the ways in which Gabriel's consciousness is presented in the story, see Riquelme, 120-30.

[9] Ellmann, 258.

[10] Beck, 358.

[11] Whether at the end of the story Gabriel remains one of the Dublin's living-dead, is changed, or on the verge of change after a redemptive experience, continues to be argued. Among recent optimistic views are those of Marilyn French, "Missing Pieces in Joyce's *Dubliners*," *Twentieth Century Literature* 24 (Winter, 1978): 465-71; Joanne Higgins, "A Reading of the Last Sentence in 'The Dead'" *English Language Notes* 17 (1980): 203-07; John D. Boyd, "Gabriel Conroy's Secret Sharer," *Studies in Short Fiction* 17 (Fall, 1980): 499-501; Robert Boyle, "Ellmann's Revised Conroy," *James Joyce Quarterly* 21 (Spring, 1984): 257-64; and, among the more pessimistic on this point, Donald T. Torchiana, "The Ending of 'The Dead': I Follow St. Patrick," *James Joyce Quarterly* 18 (1981): 123-32, and Mary T. Reynolds, *Joyce and Dante* (Princeton: Princeton University Press, 1981), 161-62. Zack Bowen, "Joyce and the Epiphany Concept: A New Approach," *Journal of Modern Literature* 9, 1 (1981-82): 109-10, argues that the final paragraph of the story has more of Gabriel's overripe language in composing a romantic scene (as with the picture of Gretta as "Distant Music") than the convincing resonance of real insight and change of heart, and a similar view is taken by David Shields, "A Note on the Conclusion of Joyce's 'The Dead,'" *James Joyce Quarterly* 22 (Summer, 1985): 427-28. A middle course is taken by Gregory Lucente, "Encounters and Subtexts in 'The Dead': A Note on Joyce's Narrative Technique," *Studies in Short Fiction* 20 (Fall, 1983): 281-87, who argues that the "story's subtexts, unperceived by the character, undermine the integrity of Gabriel's consciousness and permit the narrative to depict

the limits of his realizations from within as well as from without, creating the aesthetic distance of irony even during the story's moments of greatest sympathy."

D. H. Lawrence:
The Secrets of
"The Rocking-Horse Winner"

    Lawrence's "Rocking-Horse Winner" is a fable about a family whose struggle to keep up social appearances causes it to fail terribly in more important human values. The exposition presents a mother who begins with "all the advantages" but whose unlucky secret is that she loves neither her husband nor her children; a shadowy and distant father whose prospects never materialize; and three children who are haunted by the insistent but unspoken need in the home for more money. The statement of the problems ends as the boy Paul, after naively questioning his mother about the family's poor luck, begins a search for the solution which has eluded his parents.
    The boy's search is inspired by conversations with the gardener Bassett about horse races. But Paul's search is his own secret, a mysterious and frantic effort to predict winners of the races and, with Bassett's help, bet accordingly. When skeptical Uncle Oscar quietly investigates, he

finds that the boy has already had substantial success. Ignoring the child's growing nervousness, he keeps his profitable secret and joins the betting group. In contrast to his parents, however, Paul manages his finances prudently and is thus able to provide some secret support to his mother.

With carefully controlled suspense, Paul's luck is continued but is threatened by some losses, the increasing strain on his health, and the growing concern of his mother, who finally threatens to send him off to the seaside to rest. Separation from his rocking-horse, the secret source of his luck, is avoided, but at the cost finally of sacrificing Paul to his mania. Only at the climax does the mother show real love for her son. But, after the accumulation of secret mistrust and exploitation, her concern is tragically too late.

As the story moves through its series of secrets, then, it becomes a successful combination of the flatness of fable and melodrama and the pregnancy of symbolic realism. The achievement owes much to the insistent rhythms of the developing suspense and the mysterious images of the rocking-horse itself, the mother's stony heart, the child's burning eyes.

D. H. Lawrence's "The Rocking-Horse Winner" is a fable about a beautiful mother who had no luck, her young son who did, and the consequent rise and fall of their fortunes. It is a story of unusual power, with a skillfully managed plot line that rises to a dramatic climax and denouement. The "moral" of the fable has several targets: living beyond one's means; the consequent anxiety about money that diminishes genuine life; the failure of selfish adults in meeting the needs of a well-meaning but confused child; the appearances of trust and love compared to the reality.

The omniscient, detached, but aggressively ironic narrator begins the story in simple fable style: "There was a woman who was beautiful, who started with all the advantages, yet she had no luck" (790).[1] The first sentence begins two key patterns of the story, that of generalization followed by a series of specific examples and that of statements with adversative qualifications. As the specifics are presented in the first paragraph, the sentences rock back and forth between the appearances of luck or good fortune and the reality of bad luck or personal failure: "She had bonny children, yet she felt they had been thrust upon her and she could not love them."

In the first four paragraphs, some of the basic disclosures are that the woman cannot love anybody—and her children read that failure in her eyes; that the family are snobbish; that they don't have enough money "though the style was always kept up"; that they don't know how to cope with their predicament. These conventional premises, however, are presented with some intensity. There are elements of violence in the tactile imagery ("thrust upon her," "a grinding sense"), of urgency ("hurriedly," "at last"), of strong feeling ("troubled," "anxious"), of complicating ignorance and incapacity ("she racked her brains", "he never would be able"). But more important are the elements of emphasis and compelling repetition. These include simple italicizing of words ("I will see if *I*," "he never *would*"); hyperbole ("all the advantages"); the use of *she* as the subject of so many sentences and clauses; the frequent use of short sentences with few if any modifiers—and the staccato rhythm that results. The most important of these emphatic and repetitive elements are the references to money which begin in the fourth paragraph presumably as the worried thought of the mother: "There must be more money, there must be more money." The sentiment is picked up by the ghostly voices of the house which are then introduced, a secret cry which the children and even their toys could hear all the time, though nobody said it aloud.

The action of the story rises from the summary of these nagging difficulties and is triggered by a dialogue between the harassed mother and her inquisitive son, now introduced as Paul. Paul is tentative and indirect, but conventionally persistent in his questions; the mother is deliberate and increasingly bitter in her answers. What she makes clear to Paul in a series of distinctions and clarifications is that, while money is important in life, luck is more important, perhaps the most important thing. Luck, she explains, is the ability to get money when it is needed. And no one knows the who and the why of luck; it is God's secret. As parental teaching of life's values this is unbalanced, but Paul accepts it as an adequate explanation of the family's difficulties and a problem he should deal with. He is intuitively certain, however, that his mother is trying to hide something else from him (her unhappiness? the failure of the marriage?), as he is sure that she does not believe and pay any attention to his sudden assertion that, even though father and mother are not, he is indeed lucky. The direction of the action is thus set: Paul must find the clue to being lucky and demonstrate to his mother that he has the secret. The direction has been set, however, only after repeated presentations of the family's problem: in impersonal narration from the mother's point of view, from the children's, from that of the family in general, from that of the house and its haunting by the voices, and, finally, in a dramatic scene, from that of Hester and Paul. And within this larger series of repetitions, the smaller elements of rhythmic insistence and emphasis are skillfully deployed.

The longest part of the story (pp. 792-97) deals with Paul's search for and rather quick discovery of luck and, then, the longer application and testing of his discovery by two of his elders. Paul's search for luck is inward, but he pursues it in wild rides on his rocking-horse. And he finds it, as the winners of coming racing events are revealed to him. In the rather public process of his initial search, a contrast is developed between Paul's silent and wild-eyed pursuit of this valuable information (the winners seem always to be at long odds) and the reactions of his nurse (who feels he has grown beyond her), his sisters (who are afraid and want him to stop his noisy rides), his mother (who watches him with anxious expression), and Uncle Oscar (who encourages the young sportsman). Given the violence and obsessiveness of the boy's play ("he would slash the horse", "if only he forced it"), it is already clear that the reaction of the elders is inadequate. But nothing is done. It is clear, too, that Paul's toy has been brilliantly chosen as the central symbol of the story—and has been neatly introduced with the listening toys in the exposition, before its special powers are even hinted at.

Once Paul has found luck, the use of his knowledge in betting is introduced immediately (794), but then tested at length through the amused and sceptical inquiries of Oscar Cresswell with Bassett, twice with Paul, twice with Paul and Bassett, and again with Paul. This series has the advantage of modulating the fable into a more realistic base during the rising action. For indeed the story welds two narrative styles and levels of credibility—and the transitions are made especially through skeptical Uncle Oscar. While his careful inquiries brake the headlong movement of the plot (and, like Paul's occasional failures on the rocking-horse, thereby add to the suspense), they also show that Oscar is more concerned about the value of Paul's tips than about the advisability of the boy's involvement.

The unusual partnership which Oscar is eventually happy to join is characterized, of course, by secrecy and the code of honor. But the new relationships are defined more dramatically by forms of reference and address. A contrast is developed, that is, between the authoritative address of Mother and Nanny to Paul (as well as the narrator's references to "the boy" and "the child") and the religious awe of Bassett and his properly respectful "Master Paul." And in the same respectful pattern are the joshing and embarrassed indirection of Oscar's "old man," "laddie," "son," "sonny," and "young jockey." There is much respect, therefore, for Paul's inside information, but not enough concern for the danger his mother will later point out to him and then proceed to ignore herself.

If the imprudence and uncaring blindness of the elders is judged strongly throughout the story, the judgment falls more lightly and ambivalently on the mother, Hester. For she is indeed, by Oscar's acquiescence to Paul, kept in the dark to the very end about what is really going on. What is weighed against Oscar's duty to his sister is Paul's desire to have his powers remain a secret (lest mother stop him), his wish to help her financially and exorcise the house of its whispers (but anonymously)—and, of course, Oscar's self-interest in the arrangement.

The rise to the climax of the story begins immediately after Paul's secret gift is received so coldly by his mother, she successfully wrangles the whole trust fund, and proceeds to squander it. It is then that the "voices in the house suddenly went mad . . . trilled and screamed in a sort of ecstasy: 'There *must* be more money!'" (800). With Paul's losing in the next two races and becoming "wild-eyed and strange, as if something were going to explode in him," even Oscar admonishes him not to bother with the business, and his mother "looks at him anxiously, her heart curiously heavy because of him." But after his objections and pleadings, she does not pursue the obviously prudent course of getting him away. There is finally her rather fatuous request, "Promise us you won't let your nerves go to pieces" (801).

The potentials for the tragic conclusion and its enlarged symbolism having thus been arranged, we are given in quick succession Hester's worry about Paul the evening she is away at a party; her phone call to the nurse, but her imprudent decision not to invade the child's privacy; after some suspenseful moments before his door, the dramatic discovery of his mad ride on the rocking-horse and then his collapse. And "she, all her tormented motherhood flooding upon her, rushed to gather him up" (803). Her reaction sounds like the first flowering of real maternal love, but immediately thereafter Hester is "heart-frozen" and sits "stonily" at Paul's bedside. Perhaps, even the threat of his death is insufficient to change Hester or after this one moment, the guilt of her failure in responsibility or the realization of her final misfortune has turned her heart "actually into a stone" (804).

The denouement uses Bassett to announce Malabar's victory and Paul finally to explain before he dies the secret of his inspiration and the motives of his obsessive efforts to achieve it. These motives were not simply to help his mother or still the whispering of the house, but also it would seem, to prove his importance to his mother, to have her attention and her love: "Don't you think I'm lucky, mother . . . Mother, did I ever tell you? I *am* lucky."

Two bits of irony close the story. Answering Paul's question, his mother says, "No, you never did." Paul, of course, had told her in the triggering dialogue of the action that he was lucky and that God had told him so. The implication here seems to be that he never told Hester what he had just offered as the real explanation of his luck, that she had, therefore, been left in the dark.

The second remark is Oscar's and it returns the story to its beginning: with such large winnings Hester appears to be quite lucky, but in reality she has had the worst luck—the sacrifice of the son she seemed at last capable of loving.

Critics have been at pains to demonstrate that the meanings of the story are more complex than this sketch would suggest. They relate the themes traced here to some of the persistent ideas of Lawrence's fiction arguing, for example, that Paul's tragedy results from the unspoken demands of "the devouring mother"[2] or from the weakness of a father who, as a poor provider, creates the conditions for greed in the family and the death of his wife's heart, a death mystically echoing Paul's.[3] Many critics relate the anxious life of the family to the emotion-drained and cramped existence of modern man that concerned Lawrence. Thus, for W. R. Martin, the *wooden* horse that rocks back and forth without getting anywhere is a good symbol for the diminished life of the family:

> The real and lively race-horses, whose names—Sansovino, Daffodil, Lancelot, Mirza, Singhalese, Blush of Dawn, Lively Sparks—resound insistently through the story, represent with almost crude emblematic clarity the possibilities in a fully lived life and one in ironic contrast to the wooden horse, which, with its "springs," "mechanical gallop" and "arrested prance" is a symbol of the unlived, merely mimetic, life of Paul's parents.[4]

Other analysts note that Paul withdraws from the life of the family and that there is a strong implication that his riding is sexual and onanistic.[5] Moreover, since his obsessive ritual yields special knowledge and power, some suggest a pact between Paul and supernatural beings; in the tradition of such pacts, his death comes as retribution.[6] In a line more typical of Lawrence, it is similarly observed that Paul represents over-intellectualized modern man, who in his hubris is chasing something "which will destroy him if he ever catches it."[7] In a quite different direction, since the title of the story indicates that Paul is a "winner," his effort to save his mother can be construed (despite the oedipal elements of the situation) as an heroic exercise and his death as redemptive.[8] While some of these meanings can be comfortably accommodated to one another, the full elaboration of any one, however, fits rather awkwardly with the simplicities of the literal narrative—especially where the figure of Paul is concerned. Child characters, in general, seem resistant to heroic and tragic symbolization.

If "The Rocking-Horse Winner" cannot be characterized accurately, then, by a summary theme—Gordon and Tate's "the boy, Paul, has invoked strange gods and pays the penalty with his death"[9] or even Lawrence's own related proverb "lucky in money, unlucky in love"[10]—neither can its success be adequately explained by the quantity, indirection, or complexity of its meanings. The search should rather be in the interaction of these elements:

> A satisfactory analysis must be one which responds to the way in which Lawrence has woven together character and symbol, theme and plot tension. These elements do not exist separately, they must be seen in relationship to each other.[11]

If the story, then, is about lucky and unlucky people; about keeping up appearances and the anxieties attendant on that effort; about the appearance of love and its reality, selfishness and self-sacrifice; about parapsychological or magical knowledge and its ultimate physical and moral cost; about child's play and adult sport, children's needs and adult unconcern—these diverse elements, it should be observed, are developed within a suspenseful narrative about a family group. In the group, each person has his or her aspirations, frustrations, and, especially, secrets—and each is affected by Paul's probing of the most basic secret, his exploiting it with several of the others and then suffering its final recompense. A basic tension in the situation, therefore, is that of finding and using some secrets, of keeping others.

Paul is, thus, at the center of a group among whom relationships are familial and cordial, but are more basically wary, uncertain and secretive. While everyone, for example, says that Hester "adores her children," she and the children know the secret that this is not so; they read it in one another's eyes. The children know among themselves that each of them has heard the secret whispering in the house, though it is unspoken. God, says mother, knows but never tells why some people are lucky and others are not. From the lines of her mouth, Paul knows that his mother "was only trying to hide something from him." Bassett doesn't want to give Paul away to Oscar, and when Uncle Oscar sounds Paul out, the "boy watched the handsome man closely" and "parried" his questions. The secret of the partnership must be maintained as a matter of "honor." The source of the gift to mother must be a secret. The "secret of secrets" has been hinted at sufficiently (we don't, in what is the story's biggest flaw, need to be told directly before the climax that it "was his wooden horse" [801]) to develop the dramatic irony of Hester's ignorance as the climax approaches—and Paul finally reveals to her the secret of his luck.

Paul is the center of unity in this series of secrets, his own secret struggle directed within and above (at luck, fortune, a secretive God) as well as without (to the recalcitrant horse, the tool of his efforts). It is specifically the successes and failures of this struggle that affect those around him and determine the action of the story. This tight focus on "the rocking-horse winner" himself makes for unusual intensity as the consequent pressure and suspense of the horse races and the bets on long-shots also begin to affect the group.

And the developing action, most commentators agree, is pursued with a leanness and tautness unusual in Lawrence: short sentences, short paragraphs, brief but insistent repetitions. There are crisp junctures and transitions between an unusually large number of scenes and narrative summaries for the length of the story.[12] A single sentence from Paul's older sister, for example, introduces Bassett and his conversations with the boy about racing. But speed in the action is of no particular value in itself. It is rather the fact that here it is in good balance with the development of plausibility for the "uncanny" elements of the story. While Bassett may need only a sentence of preparation, the rocking-horse gets a much more careful and gradual introduction.

The balance of narrative speed and the more leisurely provisions for plausibility is paralleled and overlapped by another successful fusion—the combination of fable style, which dominates especially the beginning, and the realistic style of other stretches of the narrative. This is a matter of characterization as much as the style of convincing dialogue or narrative summary: the husband, nurse, sisters never move from the flatness and sketchiness of fable, but Uncle Oscar, clearly of the men's club and race track, helps Hester and Paul to straddle both worlds.

Some analysts might argue, however, that none of the characters moves beyond the flatness of art deco illustrations (though with Claude Lovatt Fraser and others, that can be attractive), and that the most complex and interesting nodes of meaning are the symbols. A good case could certainly be made for the rocking-horse; it rather neatly interfaces the world of child's play with the deadly excitement and seriousness of adult sport and gambling—and figures prominently in the secrets, the casuality and motivations of the story. But other symbols—the stony-heart and burning eyes—seem more mechanical and obtrusive in their repetitions, less complex in their functional relationships.

In the final analysis, what seems most admirable is the pacing of the story and the steady and even emergence of thematic patterns, especially the ironies, as the action develops. There is the irreversible increase of pressures as the financial situation worsens and Paul must work more feverishly to come up with winners. There is, to repeat, the setting of this basic action in a network of secrecy and wariness, beneath a calmer surface of maternal solicitude and friendly joviality. The general tempo of the rising action is accelerated at times by the rapid turnover of scenes or by insistent repetitions; it is delayed at times by the investigations of Oscar or the failures of Paul—and its suspense thereby increased; it is relaxed at other times, as in Paul's second lengthy dialogue with his mother and his urging her not to worry.[13]

The developing ironies of the story also succeed for the most part, whether the pains to keep up the appearance of comfort; the primacy given to luck in the life of a family; the dominating role of the child in the fortunes of his elders or their lack of perceptiveness in dealing with his sensitivities. And these elements are neatly brought together in the discovery and reversal of the climax—and the concluding judgments of Hester and Oscar.

One cannot fully account, of course, for *all* of the critical choices that have been made in smaller and larger structures of the story. They range from the proper name for a horse, the number of times the ghostly whisperers will repeat their warning, the flattening or rounding of a character, the dramatizing of the climax, the pacing of an episode or the whole plot. But Lawrence seems more often than not to have responded correctly to the multiple demands of his developing story, to have achieved here a "true unweighted conflict, an exploration, not an assertion."[14]

Notes

[1] Page references in parentheses are to *D. H. Lawrence: The Complete Short Stories*, Vol III (London: Heineman, 1970), 790-804.

[2] Donald Junkins, "The Rocking-Horse Winner: A Modern Myth," *Studies in Short Fiction* 2 (1964): 87-89.

[3] Charles Koban, "Allegory and the Death of the Heart in 'The Rocking-Horse Winner,'" *Studies in Short Fiction* 15 (1978): 391-96. Koban notes, for example, the parallel motifs of Hester's cold heart and Paul's burning eyes which at the climax both turn to stone.

[4] W. R. Martin, "Fancy or Imagination? 'The Rocking-Horse Winner,'" *College English* 24 (1962): 64-65. This and some fourteen other papers on Lawrence's story have been conveniently reprinted in Dominick P. Consolo, ed., *The Rocking-Horse Winner* (Columbus, Ohio: Merrill, 1969). For a detailed and imaginative analysis of the names of characters and horses, see Hugh H. Ingrasci, "Names as Symbolic Crowns Unifying Lawrence's 'The Rocking-Horse Winner,'" *Festchrift in*

Honor of Virgil V. Vogel, ed. Edward Callary (Dekalb, Ill.: Illinois Name Society, 1985), 1-22.

[5]W. D. Snodgrass, "A Rocking-Horse: The Symbol, the Pattern, Way to Live," *The Hudson Review* 11, No. 2 (1958): 191-200 (also in Consolo): "Just as the riding of a horse is an obvious symbol for the sex act, and 'riding' was once the common sexual verb, so the rocking-horse stands for the child's imitation of the sex act, for the riding which goes nowhere" (196).

[6]Caroline Gordon and Allen Tate, *The House of Fiction* (New York: Scribner, 1960), 227-30. However, V. J. Emmet, Jr., "Structural Irony in D. H. Lawrence's 'The Rocking-Horse Winner,'" *The Connecticut Review* 5, No. 2 (1972): 5-10, argues that there is no indication of such dealings in the story and that the powers of the rocking-horse are related rather to fairy tales in which animals bring good luck to their owners. Other aspects of the "uncanny" elements of the story are offered by James G. Hepburn, "Discovery and Uncanny Visions; Freud's 'The Uncanny' with Regard to Form and Content in Stories by Sherwood Anderson and D. H. Lawrence," *Literature and Psychology* 9 (1959): 9-12, and W. S. Marks III, "The Psychology of the Uncanny in Lawrence's 'The Rocking-Horse Winner,'" *Modern Fiction Studies* 9 (1965-66): 381-92 (both in Consolo).

[7]Snodgrass, 195.

[8]Frederick W. Turner, III, "Prancing in to a Purpose: Myths, Horses, and True Selfhood in Lawrence's 'The Rocking-Horse Winner,'" (in Consolo, 95-106).

[9]Gordon and Tate, 230.

[10]Kingsley Widmer, *The Art of Perversity* (Seattle: University of Washington Press, 1962), 92 (the full analysis is excerpted in Consolo).

[11] Rory Lamson, Hallett Smith, Hugh Maclean, Wallace W. Douglas, *The Critical Reader* (New York: W. W. Norton, 1962), 547 (also in Consolo).

[12] Emmet, 6.

[13] Emmet, 9, suggests that this dialogue fulfills the function of the fourth act of classical tragedy, to provide "a decent interval of time so that the catastrophe does not follow too closely upon the crisis."

[14] Mark Kincaid-Weekes, "The Marble and the Statue: The Exploratory Imagination of D. H. Lawrence," in *Imagined Worlds: Essays on English Novels and Novelists in Honour of John Butt*, ed. Ian Gregor and Maynard Mack (London: Methuen, 1968), 385.

Katherine Mansfield: Mansfield's "The Fly" and The Vulnerable Boss

Mansfield's "The Fly" combines three episodes which seem quite disparate because very different actions and secondary characters are involved. Each episode, however, is a variation on a situation in which the boss dominates the other character but in the process reveals his own illusions and weaknesses. With old Woodifield, he is the vigorous business leader who needs his weekly meed of adulation; in his memories of his long-dead son, he is still the aggrieved parent who thinks of himself as the more tragic figure; with a fly struggling in an ink blot on his desk, he is the obstinate examiner of its will to survive and the strangely frightened witness of its failure. In each case, his attempts to assert himself end in frustration but do not bring him closer to reality.

The connections between these thematically related parts, however, are shaky at several points, particularly in the transition to the more heavily symbolic third section. While the combination of a realistic account with elements *of parable and exemplum is not unusual, the effect here is of individually strong renderings of the main character but in quite different styles. The story ends with a brief coda that repeats the contrast between strength and weakness, the boss bullying a subordinate but having an ambiguous lapse of memory.*

If "The Garden Party" represents a high point in Mansfield's powers of lyrical evocation, "The Fly" (1922) represents the final achievement of the ironic and satiric talents that were shown early, if rather crudely, in her first book, *In a German Pension* (1911). But the story is not without its problems, and analysts have had particular difficulty in showing how the three parts of the story interrelate and how they are consistent in theme and narrative style. For while the story is not unusual in combining a realistic account with elements of the parable and exemplum, the relation of these factors is not always clear. The minor characters, for instance,—and the office messenger Macey should be included—serve the exemplary functions of the narrative simply by their flatness. But the nameless boss, at the center of its moral concerns, is a shifting complex of opposed traits. He is, by turns, stern and kind; conscious of his superiority and even contemptuous of others, but, in some circumstances, sympathetic and even admiring of them. He can be quite definite and assertive; at other times, he is puzzled and uncertain. He is selfish, manipulating others to satisfy his own feelings. And in pursuing these satisfactions, he is misguided, persistently avoiding the evidence that these pleasures must end, even his most basic pleasure in being boss. He is, then, not simply the strong man in public who in private proves to be weak, but he is also a victim of his complex self-deception. In particular, he refuses to see when it is and is not reasonable to persist, and he is finally left in a search for happiness which, as it is soon to end, seems all the more pitiably astray.

The first episode is concerned with satisfactions that seem rather minor, but it deals too with what lurks as the threat to them. The story opens with a primary contrast between the apparent comfort and security of the boss's situation and the diminished satisfactions left to old Woodifield since his retirement, "since . . . his stroke." Having lost his strength, the old man is now descending into his second childhood, dressed and brushed by his wife and daughters and set free only on Tuesdays to bother his friends back in the City. "Y'are very snug in here," pipes old Mr. Woodifield to the boss, with some enthusiasm but also with the note immediately of confinement that will run through the story.

By contrast, the boss is "stout, rosy, five years older than he, and still going strong, still at the helm," with a hearty endurance that is clearly a major feature of his superiority. Woodifield's pleasure is simply to chat, smoke his cigar, and gaze greedily from his big chair "as a baby peers out of its pram." The boss's pleasure is simply to have Woodifield admire his office and, indeed, himself "planted there in the midst of it in full view of that frail old figure in the muffler" (597).[1] As the scene develops, however, it becomes clear that the boss takes even more pleasure in simply bossing: showing off "for the past—how many?— weeks" the improvements to the office; ignoring the family prohibition of whiskey to old Woodifield; telling him indeed how he should drink it.

The contrast between the two men is thus developed consistently, even in this minor key, as between strong and weak, especially in references to quick and robust, as opposed to slow and uncontrolled, movement. The boss flips, nods, moves, winks, unlocks, draws forth, swoops, pours, tosses off, while more typically his ailing friend pipes (a shade too often, perhaps), trembles, grows dim, speaks faintly, lets his mouth fall open in surprise, almost cries, forgets, quivers, pauses, shuffles. Their common pleasures, however, are presented only in strong terms: the office rug is *bright* red with *large* white circles, the bookcase is *massive*, the whiskey is *beautiful* and *rare*, especially tempting since it has been forbidden by misguided women and offered by a man of experience. These satisfactions are also colored by a Dickensian geniality and humor: table legs like twisted treacle, electric heating elements like pearly sausages, the boss *cocking* an eye at Woodifield (the name itself seems borrowed), the old man rolling his whiskey in his *chaps*.[2] And, not surprisingly, the idea of satisfaction and attachment is expressed as simple and plain desire: "he liked to have it admired . . . I wanted to tell you . . . I thought you'd like to know . . . he liked a nice broad path."

But frequent time references emphasize that Woodifield's happy experience is brief and uncertain, reluctantly concluding for the present, soon to end completely. For he is "on his last pins." Now his "talk is over; it was time for him to be off. But he did not want to go." For, says the narrator rather too directly, "we cling to our last pleasures as the tree clings to its last leaves" (597). If terminal illness and death is thus the immediate threat to Woodifield's small satisfactions, death in another guise is now introduced as more immediately affecting the boss's more comprehensive and private pleasures and attachments. Against the ground of prosperity, vigorous health, current improvements, the first dark note comes with the picture above the table. Woodifield is not asked to notice it; it is not new, not an improvement. The note passes, but it returns after the boss keeps Woodifield on for the whiskey, expanding in Woodifield's enthusiastic report on the Belgian cemetery where both their sons are buried. While Woodifield expatiates on the beauty of the cemetery, its careful tending, its wide paths—and, not so inconsequentially, on the banal details of how the Belgians exploit the feelings of visitors—the boss remains silent. His only movement is now like one of Woodifield's, "a quiver in his eyelids." He is clearly disturbed.

Just how and why this can be so is the matter of the second episode, the episodes themselves, large as they are, presenting themselves as the functioning units of the structure in which we are most conscious of balances and contrasts. Thus it is that his orders to Macey for complete privacy, as he shuts himself in the office, and even the methodic way he addresses his grief, continue the strength of the boss's characterization. But now the bullying man is about to weep, and the feelings he controlled in the presence of Woodifield are about to overcome him. What seems to be a complete reversal, however, is not really that, for even in his grief the boss has established his superiority. Unlike the grief of Woodifield and others—common, publicly discussed, adjusted to in time—the boss's mourning is exclusive, private, persevering. For his loss, he tells himself, is unique: an only son, whose magnificent promise was just about to be fulfilled, has been cut off. From there it is a short step to the even more important source of his grief—not the loss of a child as such, but of parental expectations for him. As with Shaw's boss, Andrew Undershaft, succession to the family business is of overriding importance, and so typical clichés of the situation like "learning the ropes" or "stepping into his shoes" take on additional overtones of control by the father-figure here. With the collapse of his essential hope, the boss has nothing left. His sentimental, ritualized mourning begins with him staring at "nothing," insisting that "nobody, nobody at all" is to see him. He concludes by telling himself that everything he had "slaved, denied himself, kept going" for has disappeared, is "over and done with as though it has never been," that with his son's death, the whole place simply "crashed about his head," that he was "a broken man, with his life in ruins."

Despite this excess of self-pity and the obvious contrast with the current picture of the boss as prosperous and thriving, the final irony is that the rite of grief he has morbidly persisted in for years, now fails to produce the tears he "wanted, he intended, he had arranged for" (600). Thus, if the persistence of desire and attachment dominates the first episode, their frustration dominates the second. That frustration, moreover, is a judgment on the unreasonableness of the boss's persistence in his grief and the emptiness of his rationalizations about it. He had thought of himself as a strong and nobly tragic figure, but he reveals himself as deluded and weak, indulging long past sorrows far from unique, enjoying the success and material rewards of a business far from ruined.

While other balances, ironic contrasts, and motivations between the two episodes seem clear enough, we may well ask what has caused the "failure" of his emotional catharsis now. It may be the unexpectedness of Woodifield's story ("a terrible shock" to the boss), but it seems also to have been the first image that suggested itself to him thereafter: "It was exactly as though the earth had opened and he had seen the boy lying there with Woodifield's girls staring down at him" (600). What has upset and disoriented the boss is this "opening" of the closed grave, this violation of his privacy and his control of his son in death as he had controlled him in life. And the photograph he now has recourse to cannot erase the frustrating effect of the earlier image. For the photograph does not gee with the more pleasant memories he has persisted in, despite the changes the war had brought and which are now reflected in the "cold, even stern-looking" expression of the young man in the photo.[3]

It is just at the moment the son's picture is being used as another possible means to catharsis that the boss is distracted by the fly caught in the ink pot and he rescues it. He begins to admire the insect's spunky effort to clean itself from the ink, until the "horrible danger was over, it has escaped, it was ready for life again." But just then the boss has a new idea: wet the fly with another drop of ink and see how it reacts. The reaction is the same, and in two such drowning tests the fly recovers as the boss's admiration increases for "the plucky little devil . . . the artful little b . . . " But the boss persists unreasonably with a third test and just as unreasonably is disappointed when the fly succumbs on the soaked blotting paper of his desk:

> "Come on," said the boss. "Look sharp!" And he stirred it with his pen—in vain. Nothing happened or was likely to happen. The fly was dead. (602)

The boss's frustration is elaborated in the conclusion. He flings "the corpse" away, is frightened by a "grinding feeling of wretchedness," calls sternly to the old dog Macey for clean blotting paper, finally wonders what he had been thinking about before.

Each of the story's three parts, therefore, details in several stages not simply the boss's domination of the character he interacts with but also the way he seeks his own satisfaction. In each instance his search is frustrated. The pleasures of a chat with an admiring friend are ruined by Woodifield's report about the cemetery. The end result is anything but right, but in his confusion the boss cries "Quite right, quite right! . . . though what was quite right he hadn't the least idea" (599). The indulgence of his griefs also goes awry. "Something seemed to be wrong with him. He wasn't feeling as he wanted to feel" (601). Finally, his spirits are raised by the "never say die" effort of the fly, but dashed when it succumbs, so that he feels wretched and frightened.

How that could possibly be and how, therefore, the third part of the story functions with the first two has been argued extensively over the last thirty-five years or more. It may be that the boss's testing of the fly symbolizes the role of a cruel fate with the boss's son, with himself—or with the author, under the displeasure, too, of her own father.[4] Or the repeated trial may relate to Woodifield, whose retirement, bereavement, stroke, perhaps even the smothering care of his family have led him to his present state of death-in-life.[5] Or it may be that the killing of the fly represents "the murderous finality with which other lives are wrecked by powers indifferent to any sorrow but their own."[6] Or it may be that the death of the fly represents the end of the boss's "undying" grief, gradually weakened by his better spirits and now concluded with a wrench.[7] Or that the boss has finally an insight into his own mortality or of the transitory nature of his most basic attachments.[8]

The last suggestions, of course, are the most consonant with the narrative structure as I have described it here. The messages of mortality, that is, have been clear and they have been frequent: the weekly visits of an old man "on his last pins"; the death of sons recalled, as their cemetery is described; the killing of a fly which has just been cleaning its wing methodically with its leg "as the stone goes over and under the scythe" (601). Yet one is reluctant to rule out other possible relations. After all, the chief value of a symbol in a literary structure is its richness and complexity—as well as the natural and inevitable way it relates to other parts of the structure. One wonders, however, whether the multiplicity of suggestions here does not derive simply from the general, perhaps I should say the ultimate, nature of the meanings involved; life and death, suffering and destiny, authority and dependence involve everyone in the story, and so no one interpretation of the fly can be completely exclusive or, perhaps, can even be shown to be clearly emphasized.

However, I would be less concerned with the details or the rigorous consistency of symbolic readings than with the kind of transition between the first two parts and the third and with other problems at the close of the story. It is fair to say, for example, that the first two parts provide little preparation for the much denser implication of the third. There are, of course, the generic names of boss (repeated, in fact, some twenty-five times) and son—and the flatness of other characters. But now the formulaic repetition of the fly's testing and, more particularly, the introductory time specifications ("At that moment" and "just then") indicate that the new episode is not simply an echo of the earlier situations but is somehow a commentary on or a generalization of them, a system of a different order which is heavily, if not strictly, symbolic. The transition, then, is sharper than expected. And the motivation at this juncture is also different. The time specifications suggest that it is accidental that the fly should appear just "at this moment" (in what seems, incidentally, to be winter) and that "just then" the boss should be inspired to test its strength after its first mischance.[9] Since the fly is adventitious, then, it seems to bear a heavier "symbolic weight" than it should,[10] and the suspicion grows that its significance does not so much grow out of the first two episodes but is imposed *ex machina*, is contrived.

Moreover, while the symbolism of the fly projects backwards in complicated ways, it also inspires, even more problematically, the intense reaction of the boss at the conclusion. The boss's wretchedness and fright, of course, could possibly result simply from the fly's death—after, that is, the show of bravery which had so excited the experimenter. But the result would surely, then, be excessive. So we are left with the range of symbolic meanings, one or more of which the boss reacts to—the workings of a cruel fate and so forth. And somewhere between an immediately realistic cause and a deeper symbolism he reads in the fly's death, it may be that the boss now finally sees the deadening effect of his bossiness and the irony of his applauding the "never say die" spirit of a mere fly when he could not muster the same spirit in his great trial. Again, such complexity is fair enough in the symbolic game—and, within bounds, anything portentous enough will do, if it convincingly motivates the extreme result in the boss's feelings at the conclusion.

But another ambiguity now follows in the conclusion, and it makes for another shaky transition, an ambiguity of a different kind. For the life of him, the boss cannot remember what he was thinking of *before*. Is that when he was frustrated in his ritual of grief, when he was deciding he didn't like his son's photograph, when he was testing the fly, when he reacted to its death? This uncertainty in a simple reference to the story's time frame, coming after the accumulated ambiguities of the story, may be a bit too much, may go beyond the demand of a good impressionist artist that we make our own connections.

Whatever serious meaning the fly carries and whatever the precise nature of the boss's reaction to it, they would not seem to have affected any basic change of character. For throughout the story the boss has been side-stepping the serious issues. When Woodifield describes the cemetery, he seems not to hear: "Only a quiver in his eyelids showed that he heard." When he is confronted with the changed appearance of his son in the photograph, he is easily distracted by the fly. When he is deeply disturbed at the fly's death, he flings the dead insect away and calls for action in the office. At the end, then, he is back to bossing in his worst mode.

And with this climactic avoidance and final twist, the judgment on him is driven neatly home. It is softened, of course, by earlier touches of geniality and kindness, by the general pathos of his troubles, by the final reversal which has him forgetting like Woodifield.[11] But mixed though it is of pity and scorn, it is a strong judgment.

The completed portrait, then, has some variety and depth. Its psychology is convincing, particularly in dealing with the power of fantasy and the tenacity of attachments. Its language, too, is impressive and consistent in its imagistic immediacy, its accuracy in conveying feeling and the hesitations of reflection. Some of the comparisons attempted—including that of the scythe sharpening—are awkward, the emphasis of double and triple phrasing wears thin at times, but the modulations to free indirect discourse are managed well.

What we have finally is a well-developed triptych of a man who is simply "boss"; who is, however, not really in control of situations but is frustrated by them; who, despite his geniality and occasional kindness, is a bully who persists in the pursuit and protection of his own satisfactions—even to the point of unreasonableness; who then avoids the serious implications of the frustrations he has brought on himself, especially the inevitable truth that soon he will be boss no longer. But if the portrait is impressive, particularly in its chiaroscuro of strength and weakness, of vitality and hopelessness, there remains something awry. I have suggested here that the fault is in the conjunction of the major parts of the structure, in their alignment and in the contrast of their textures, of thinner and denser implication. It is as if the first two poses of the boss in his self-revelation are sketches in black and white, only the third in color. Mansfield has missed here the smooth blend of the symbolic and the "real" that Lawrence, say, brings off in "The Rocking-Horse Winner" or Flannery O'Connor in "The Artificial Nigger." She has, however, exercised in a significant way what Katherine Anne Porter called "a certain grim quiet ruthlessness of judgment, an unsparing and sometimes cruel eye, a natural malicious wit, an intelligent humor; and beyond all . . . a burning, indignant heart that was capable of great compassion."[12]

Notes

[1] Page references in parentheses are to *The Short Stories of Katherine Mansfield*, ed. John Middeton Murray (New York: Knopf, 1954).

[2] On Mansfield's appreciation of Dickens, see Edward Wagenknecht, *Dickens and the Scandalmongers* (Norman: University of Oklahoma Press, 1965), 99-108.

[3] This is among other interesting observations in one of the more comprehensive explications of the story, Pauletter Michel-Michot, "Katherine Mansfield's 'The Fly': An Attempt to Capture the Boss," *Studies in Short Fiction* 11 (1974): 85-92.

[4] See Willis D. Jacobs, "Mansfield's 'The Fly,' *Explicator* 5 (1947), Item 32.

[5] J. D. Thomas, "Symbol and Parallelism in 'The Fly,'" *College English* 22 (1961): 256, 260-61.

[6] Thomas Bledsoe, "Mansfield's 'The Fly,' *Explicator* 5 (1947), Item 53.

[7] Sylvia Berkman, *Katherine Mansfield: A Critical Study* (New Haven: Yale University Press, 1951), 195, and Stanley B. Greenfield, "Mansfield's 'The Fly,'" *Explicator* 17 (1958), Item 2.

[8] Thomas J. Assad, "Mansfield's 'The Fly'" *Explicator* 14 (1955), Item 10 and Clinton W. Oleson, "'The Fly' Rescued," *College English* 22 (1961): 585-86.

[9] See Richard F. Petersen, "The Circle of Truth: the Stories of Katherine Mansfield and Mary Lavin," *Modern Fiction Studies* 24 (1978-1979): 385.

[10] The phrase is from Mary H. Rohrberger, *The Art of Katherine Mansfield* (Ann Arbor: University Microfilms International, 1977), 109.

[11] The modulation of feeling for and against the boss is argued at some length by F. W. Bateson and others in "Katherine Mansfield's 'The Fly': A Critical Experience," *Essays in Criticism* 12 (1962): 39-53, 335-51, 448-52; Bateson also criticizes the notion that there are elements of fable or parable in the story.

[12] Katherine Anne Porter, "The Art of Katherine Mansfield," in *The Collected Essays and Occasional Essays* (New York: Delacorte Press, 1970), 50.

Katherine Anne Porter: The Contentment of "María Concepción"

In "María Concepción" Katherine Anne Porter elaborates the melodramatic situation of a betrayed and vengeful wife. What is unusual in her treatment of the familiar theme is her adroit and ironic handling of the attitudes which her heroine evokes. While at first María steadily declines in the estimation of her husband and neighbors, her bloody revenge actually begins a new ascent in their esteem. The first half of the story, thus, describes María's decline, the second half recounts how she is protected by husband and neighbors, how they accept the rough justice of her actions, how she achieves her final peace.

Her characterization, therefore, is the central focus of the story, and it develops in a repeated sequence of reactions—the contentment of an initial situation, the surprise of a betrayal, the agony which results. With several variations, this sequence is repeated in the six sections of the two major parts. By the end of her progress through these cycles, María proves to be more courageous than Juan, *more passionate than Rosa, more wise than Givens, more clever than Lupe—and so ready for her final moment of contentment.*

Katherine Anne Porter published her first short story, "María Concepción," in 1922. Since that time, it has held its own remarkably well against everything else from the hand of that remarkable writer. While the story has had a number of commentators in the intervening years, we still lack a broad and solid ground in discussing the sources of its success. But one can agree with Myron Liberman's judgment that the "exceptionally high quality of the fiction of Katherine Anne Porter is not to be accounted for entirely by historical-biographical means, by an exclusive attention to her serious and universal themes, or by an analysis of her striking use of mythic material alone. It is to be accounted for also, and in great measure, by its formal properties, verbal and rhetorical."[1]

One should, of course, construe "formal properties" to include any appropriate structuring in the story, even of phrases in larger structures like the narrator or plot that are finally unified in its total structure. It is impossible to account in analysis for the multiplicity and complexity of all such structures; one can, nevertheless, discuss many of them—and test how they, in one's experience of the whole story, contribute to its success.

In "María Concepción," Porter deals with a conventional situation of marital infidelity and of revenge by the offended wife. What is paradoxical, however, is that the self-possessed peasant girl María emerges from her bloody deed of revenge notably enhanced in the eyes of her young husband Juan (not to say of the reader also), and reconciled to the villagers she had earlier alienated. The progress to this end unfolds in six distinct parts, each set off by spacing in the text. The first three of these sections recount María's decline from the success and security we see her enjoying in the beginning; they describe the effects of Juan's betrayal and abandonment of her, the loss of her baby, and her silent withdrawal from the women of the village. The second three parts show her moving upward again, despite her dangerous confrontation by the police after the murder of her rival, Rosa; they trace the effects of her revenge and escape on Juan and the villagers but even more important, on herself. With such emphasis on impact and reaction, it seems clear that the plot is subordinate to the central characterization. The plot, that is, functions mainly to raise and lower, improve and damage, María's position amid the external conditions of her poverty, in her relationship to Juan and others and, most especially perhaps, in the arrangements she creates in her search for success—and which we see raveling and unraveling as the story proceeds. The basic unit of the story's structure, then, is not the simple betrayal that is repeated in various forms, but, as we shall see, a longer unit of unsuspecting contentment, the betrayal itself, and, finally, its agonizing impact.

It may be instructive to consider in detail how Porter creates the first stage and begins the process of decline. The opening three paragraphs are an extended description of María Concepción, careful in her way, self-controlled in postponing personal satisfaction, hard-working, but clearly committed to the norms of male dominance in her society. The element of self-control is expanded somewhat negatively with a hint of impassivity and cool detachment (as she ignores the doomed fowls she carries) but more positively with notes of admirable endurance and natural serenity:

Her straight back outlined itself strongly under her clean bright blue cotton rebozo. Instinctive serenity softened her black eyes, shaped like almonds, set far apart, and tilted a bit endwise. She walked with the free, natural, guarded ease of the primitive woman carrying an unborn child. The shape of her body was easy, the swelling life was not a distortion, but the right inevitable proportions of a woman. She was entirely contented. Her husband was at work and she was on her way to market to sell her fowls. (3)[2]

Here María Concepción successfully copes with and dominates the difficulties in life. From the beginning, these difficulties are expressed especially in the imagery of cutting and piercing (the feet of the peasants are typically affected, but body imagery in general looms large here and hereafter) and of weight (her fowls, the food basket, the unborn child she carries). Her strength and beauty is in the measured control of natural processes: walking, hungering, gazing, carrying a child, speaking, and of greater importance later, breathing. The quality of stasis, thus, becomes pivotal in María's characterization, and unguarded, restless, and reckless activity becomes the contrasting keynote of Juan and Rosa's development.

The element which is expanded in the next three paragraphs, however, is María's efficiency ("She had no time to waste.... Her husband was at work and she was on her way to market to sell her fowls"). There is also emphasis on her pride in her achievement: in her house (a hut), her youth, her piety (superior at least to some of the superstition she encounters), her energy, and her reputation. Most important is her success in arranging a marriage with Juan at a ceremony inside the church instead of the cheaper one outside.

Before María's proud achievement begins to crumble with Juan's betrayal, we are presented with a scene of even deeper physical contentment which recapitulates and climaxes her satisfaction and provides an effective contrast for the scene to follow.

> She paused on the bridge and dabbled her feet in the water, her eyes resting themselves from the sun-rays in a fixed gaze to the far-off mountains, deeply blue under their hanging drift of clouds. It came to her that she would like a fresh crust of honey. The delicious aroma of bees, their slow thrilling hum, awakened a pleasant desire for a flake of sweetness in her mouth. (4)

Several small structures should be noted here. The first is simply the color word *blue*, for cool colors are associated with María (the blue appropriate to the religious overtones of her name). On the other hand, warm colors (yellowed maguey leaves, dark red mouth, orange blur, pink-colored rebozo) are associated with Rosa and Juan. A second detail is the image of taste; similar images figure in description of intense reaction through the story. But more important than either of these images in the passage are the densely textured connotations of stasis (emphasis added): "*paused* on the bridge . . . eyes *resting* . . . in a *fixed* gaze . . . *hanging drift* of clouds . . . *slow* thrilling hum" (4). It is with measured accumulations of such minimal bits of meaning—as with most of her loose series of images: of weight, knife and thorn, heat and cold, eyes, feet, restless movement—that Porter creates the recurring moments of peace and agony in the story, supports basic contrasts between characters, or insinuates the foreshadowings and other ironies of the plot.

The moment of serenity contrasts sharply with the scenes which follow, but there are two paragraphs of transition in which connotations of stasis ("thick hedge . . . set protectingly . . . leaning jacal. . . . bound . . . roofed . . . flattened and overlapping. . . hunched . . . mound . . . hung a dusty golden shimmer of bees" [3-4]) begin to mix with those of strain and menace ("mark my child . . . peering through the crevices . . . cactus that sheered up nakedly, like bared knife blades . . . thrust into the earth" [3-4]).

The betrayal scene itself mingles playfulness and a sultry suggestiveness with minor allusions to cutting and, most important in the contrast, with a heavy concentration of reckless motion:

> A light gay scream of laughter rose from behind the hut; a man's short laugh joined it. "Ah, hahahaha!" went the voices together high and low, like a song.
>
> "So María Rosa has a man!" María Concepción stopped short, smiling, shifted her burden slightly, and bent forward shading her eyes to see more clearly through the spaces of the hedge.
>
> María Rosa ran, dodging between beehives, parting two stunted jasmine bushes as she came, lifting her knees in swift leaps, looking over her shoulder and laughing in a quivering, excited way. A heavy jar, swung to her wrist by the handle, knocked against her thighs as she ran. Her toes pushed up sudden spurts of dust, her half-raveled braids showered around her shoulders in long crinkled wisps. Juan Villegas ran after her, also laughing strangely, his teeth set, both rows gleaming behind the small soft black beard grow-

ing sparsely on his lips, his chin, leaving his brown cheeks girl-smooth. When he seized her, he clenched so hard her chemise gave way and ripped from her shoulder. She stopped laughing at this, pushed him away and stood silent, trying to pull up the torn sleeve with one hand. Her pointed chin and dark red mouth moved in an uncertain way, as if she wished to laugh again; her long black lashes flickered with the quick-moving lights in her hidden eyes. (5)

The unexpectedness and drama of the reversal here, the strong contrast with the elements of control, serenity, and seriousness in María's development, the dynamism of the prevailing imagery—all contribute significantly to the heightening necessary for this climax in the narrative.

Pitched at a higher level of emphasis is María's physical reaction to her betrayal: there is an unnatural immobility (she "did not stir or breathe for some seconds," was "unable to move" [4]) and a sharply intensified experience of heat and cold, of burdening and constricting weight, and of piercing ("Her forehead was cold, and yet boiling water seemed to be pouring slowly along her spine. An unaccountable pain was in her knees, as if they were broken" [5]; "a heavy cloud wrapped her head and bound her throat" [6]; and, again, "She burned all over now, as if a layer of tiny fig-cactus bristles, as cruel as spun glass, had crawled under her skin" [6]).

An interesting modulation occurs as the pain of heat, weight, and piercing are heightened in María's experience here. Previously such pain had been alluded to indirectly or implied, as in a sentence of the opening paragraph: "She would have enjoyed resting for a moment in the dark shade by the roadside, but she had no time to waste drawing cactus needles from her feet" (3).

Here, by contrast, the reference is as direct as the pain is intense, something María cannot cope with immediately.

When motion does return, it is in walking which, significantly, María cannot control completely but which, nevertheless, follows the habit of guarded ease: she "found herself walking onward, keeping the road without knowing it, feeling her way delicately" (6). And her walking becomes part of the continuing contrast with Juan and María, for as they moved off-stage to complete the betrayal, "Rosa balanced her jar on one hip and swung her long full petticoats with every step" and "Juan flourished his wide hat back and forth, walking proudly as a game-cock" (6).[3]

Careful modulation is evident, too, in moving from María's trauma here to her silent withdrawal in the second section of the story. There is interposed a rather subdued scene with Juan's employer, the archaeologist Givens, as she reaches her goal in that morning's walk and pursues her usual duties at the buried city. Other tasks are accomplished in this scene as well. The possibility of murderous revenge is continued as María kills one of the fowls for Givens' lunch and he comments on her cold-blooded manner; male dominance in the Latin social code is reasserted; and primitive social values and modes of rationalization are contrasted favorably with the logic of the overcivilized scientist: "She stood and regarded Givens condescendingly, that diverting white man who had no woman of his own to cook for him" (7).

This scene also establishes Givens as a more specific foil for Juan, as Rosa has already been developed as one for María. Givens represents reasonableness as opposed to Juan's passion, caution as opposed to his heedlessness, overcivilized masculinity and paternalistic indulgence as opposed to Juan's machismo and philandering; preoccupation with science as opposed to simple naturalism.4 In this contrast of values, which continues through the story, sympathy inclines to the primitives—and, perhaps, the simple opposition here of speech styles begins that process. The peppy colloquialism of Givens, with its contractions and its slang ("It gives me the creeps"), does not compare well with the polite formality of the peasants ("With your permission I will now go to market"). Involved, too, is the contrast of Givens' exuberance with María's seriousness and mysterious self-possession. A shade too much, however, for the success of María's characterization is the observation that "Her grand manner sometimes reminded him of royalty in exile" (7).

María's characterization can be seen to be drawn, therefore, from three principal directions in the first part of the story: the descriptive presentation and commentary of the narrator; the action and reaction of María herself at the level of plot; and the defining contrast of María with the men (Juan, Givens) and women (Rosa and the other villagers) around her. What is notable in the direct presentation is not simply the realistic balance of traits (for example, natural beauty, self-control, hard work *versus* pride, the possibility of a cruel vengefulness) but also the subtle shifts of perspective in the narration. There are key points, that is, where the viewpoint shifts from the omniscient narrator to María and to the villagers. "But María was always as proud as if she owned a hacienda," (4) concludes the narrator after describing María's success largely from her point of view. And the statement hovers somewhere between indirect and direct discourse, between the villagers' and the narrator's point of view. Later, in the opening of the second section, María continues the rationalization of her intended revenge against Rosa. She excuses herself, forgetting that she had not resisted Juan "even so much as María Rosa," as the omniscient narrator indicates. But then she invokes the sanction of her church wedding, "and that was a very different thing" (8). Again the source of this reflection is somewhat blurred between María and the narrator, as earlier, the remark about "that diverting white man who had no woman to cook for him . . . " (7). The net effect of these blurrings is to identify the narrator (and thence, the reader) more closely with María's values and those of the village, and this, of course, will become important in making the rough justice of the murder and María's escape from the police acceptable.

What one admires is the subtlety of the process. And the same can be said for the deployment of the image series already noted or the use of other small stylistic structures, even something as elementary as grammatical modifications. These latter, in fact, are quite interesting in themselves and interesting in the way they are distributed in the text, tending, as one might suspect, to accumulate in passages of heightened emphasis and emotive complexity. This is especially true of adjectival and adverbial phrases when two or three modifiers are employed: "treacherous curved spines," "free, natural, guarded ease," or "smiled softly, consentingly." Such phrases are even more striking when the noun or verb involved moves in the direction of metaphor: "a dusty, golden shimmer of bees," "a light gay scream of laughter," or "a sharp staccato whisper of wind." Miss Porter relies far less on explicit simile or metaphor than on such phrasing. But she places it with such uncommon care in simpler contexts that it is not obtrusive or eccentric nor does it interrupt narrative progress. Moreover, having committed herself to a device like this, she neither wears it out by repetition nor fails to achieve a certain level of quality with it. There is, in other words, a fitness of consistency across the story that she measures up to as she walks the thin line between too much and too little. In themselves, the phrases suggest unusual precision, a bit of irony, a very controlled deviation from ordinary usage.[5] But they are too frequent and too striking to justify any notion of Porter's style as very plain and simple.[6]

After the dramatic scenes of the first part of the story, it seems appropriate that the second section shift largely, though not completely, into summary narration. The section covers the months following Juan's betrayal and traces its deepened impact on María and, through her, on the villagers as well. After the departure of Juan and Rosa to the war, the latter's hard and subservient lot with the "battalion of experienced women of war" is described, as Rosa becomes, so to speak, a more mature and worthy target of María's revenge. The lengthy remainder of the section is then given over to the reactions of the villagers, especially Lupe, to María's problems. The conflict of "piety" and superstition is especially involved in these reactions as María bears her child, rejects Lupe's aid when it dies, increases her pious practices, is given what she considers treacherous praise by Lupe and proudly rejects it, and gradually withdraws from the other women. Attitudes shift from apathy or general content with the situation ("People shrugged, grinned") to qualified sympathy ("she was altogether too proud. So they pitied her"), to unease at her alienation ("all women have these troubles. Well, we should suffer together"). The final paragraph leaves María ready for the worst of her difficulties in the following section, as her reaction is described again in heightened images of pain and of menace:

> But María Concepción lived alone. She was gaunt, as if something were gnawing her away inside, her eyes were sunken, and she would not speak a word if she could help it. She worked harder than ever, and her

butchering knife was scarcely ever out of her hand. (10)

A major function of the second section of the story, therefore, is to develop some key attitudes and motivations. The impact of events on María continues as the main focus, but the basis is also laid for her eventual reconciliation with Juan, her revenge on Rosa (not simply the murder but also the adoption of the baby to replace the one lost here), and, ironically, for her defense by Lupe and the villagers. At the same time, the intensity of the first climax is relaxed, and the climb to the major climax is begun.

Even in this transition, and as preparations for succeeding events are being unobtrusively managed, a sequence of key moments is repeated, though in a minor mode and more sketchily than in the first section—the sequence, that is, of contentment-betrayal-agony. Here María's modest contentment is simply her stoic adjustment to her situation; it is followed by her sense of betrayal by Lupe and, by implication, the women of the village and then her painful withdrawal. The sequence is repeated more clearly in the following section, though, and with his return, Juan now becomes involved again. After the comic opera of his rescue and departure from jail, the settled assurance of his rationalization about his two women, we have his moment of utter satisfaction:

> It was pleasant to see himself in the role of hero to two such desirable women. He had just escaped from the threat of a disagreeable end. His clothes were new and handsome, and they had cost him just nothing. María Rosa had collected them for him here and there after battles. He was walking in the early sunshine, smelling the good smells of ripening cactus-figs, peaches, and melons, of pungent berries dangling from the pepper-

trees, and the smoke of his cigarette under his nose.
He was on the way to civilian life with his patient chief.
His situation was ineffably perfect, and he swallowed
it whole. (12)

The comedy of the opening scenes winds down now, however, as Juan in a real sense betrays himself and compounds his betrayal of María. With the heady experience of his triumphal return, the birth of his son, and the celebration in the "Death and Resurrection" pulque shop, Juan's emotions "so twisted him" that he takes leave of his "balance" and finds himself unaccountably in his own house "attempting to beat María Concepción by way of re-establishing himself in his legal household" (13). When María stands off his drunken attempt to beat her, he looks at her "inquiringly," not unlike the doomed fowl at the beginning of the story.

And indeed it is with the fowl that María begins her scene, fumbling to tie them for the market. Her panic now is the antithesis of her stately progress to market at the opening. With the sudden realization of what her problem is, her dark night of decision begins, and the major images of pain flood back, burning, constricting, immobilizing, bitter. From the darkness and her intense concentration on her bafflement come her decision and the ominously simple conclusion: "After a great while she stood up and threw the rebozo off her face, and set out walking again" (14). What impresses one here is that Porter has made such an admirable passage of comedy with Juan serve so completely the more serious moment of María's painful difficulties. At the same time, she varies the basic sequence of contentment-betrayal-agony, by shifting another element to Juan.

A more radical shift in this sequence characterizes its use in the whole second part of the story; that is, the initial element of the sequence becomes Juan's (and Rosa's) completely and it becomes the negative pole, agonizing, while the concluding element becomes María's, contentment. The distribution of these moments in the various sections of the story, therefore, could be outlined in the following fashion:

Part I	Contentment	Betrayal	Agony
Section 1	María	Juan	María
Section 2	María	Lupe	María
Section 3	Juan	Juan	María

Part II	Agony	Betrayal	Contentment
Section 4	Juan	María	María
Section 5	Rosa	Lupe	María
Section 6	Juan	Juan	María

The division of the story into the two large movements of María's decline and paradoxical rise provides the basic frame for its careful balances and contrasts. But such relations are worked out so constantly between and within individual episodes that one cannot account for them all. At the beginning of the fourth section, for example, María's betrayal of Juan, like his own of her, is played off-stage and is only to be inferred here, even in the confession. But before this betrayal is made clear, there is agony for Juan in his premonitory sleep and the mistaken fear to which he awakens. Thus while the climax resembles the one in the first section in having a discovery and a reversal of what is considered good fortune, it is complicated and intensified here by the discovery and reversal of what Juan considers a threat on his life. The familiar imagery of pain is also continued but now with Juan—the menace of cutting, for example, "the long sharpened streak of light piercing the cornhusk walls" (14); intense reaction in terms of heat and, more especially, of internal bodily sensation, e.g., "a blur of orange light seared his eyeballs . . . He tugged at the leash of his stupor . . . the hair of his head seemed to be lifting . . . felt his vitals contract . . . an enormous sigh rattled in his chest" (14-16).

For María, on the other hand, there is a steady progress to contentment again. At the moment of confession, there is neither the paralyzing immobility of her previous agonies nor yet the utter rest of peace but rather an intermediate state: fixed and rigid but also passive and dependent. Thus Juan "took her head between both his hands, and supported her in this way . . . he held her . . . stood up and dragged her up with him . . .[and she] was silent and perfectly rigid, holding to Juan with resistless strength, her hands stiffened on his arms" (14-15). Another, but not inconsistent, development in the images of stasis is the use of a huddled, bent-over posture that appears to suggest the suffering of the peasant but also a resolute accommodation to it.[7] There is in it, too, a suggestion of primitive religious meaning (explicit, of course, in María's profound and frightening obeisance to Juan in her confession). The whole scene, in fact, through the communing of husband and wife over supper is suffused with that significance. And María indicates that for her "everything is settled now" (15).

Amid the confusion and pathos of the reconciliation, Juan, as commentators have noted, reaches manhood. The change is accomplished skillfully in a few paragraphs, with, first, a rush of short narrative details and exclamations in groups of two and three:

> Then he took her head between both his hands, and supported her in this way, saying swiftly, anxiously reassuring, almost in a babble:

> "On thou poor creature! Oh madwoman! Oh, my María Concepción, unfortunate! Listen . . . .Don't be afraid. Listen to me! I will hide thee away, I thy own man will protect thee! Quiet! Not a sound!" (14)

There is then a quickly dawning sense of real danger, danger to María, which is all the more telling as it comes so soon after Juan's experience of war, the threat of a firing squad and of the knife—and the realization grows through a sequence of brief sentences about danger, narrative, expository, and finally exclamatory:

> For the first time in his life Juan was aware of danger. This was danger. María Concepción would be dragged away between two gendarmes, with him following helpless and unarmed, to spend the rest of her days in Gelen Prison, maybe. Danger! (15)

And this precipitates the imperative mode; Juan speaks typically in command for the last two-thirds of this section, as he assumes his new role as husband-protector. His commands sound sometimes like those of Lady Macbeth to her blood-smeared husband, and they contrast with the unconscious humor of his Biblical parody earlier: "I say to her, come here, and she comes straight. I say, go there, and she goes quickly" (11). But they are efficient elements in the new stage of his characterization, and they elicit the submission from María which is presented as a redemptive yet baffling revelation:

> Seating himself cross-legged near her, he stared at her as at a creature unknown to him, who bewildered him utterly, for whom there was no possible explanation . . . .He could not fathom her, nor himself, nor the mysterious fortunes of life grown so instantly confused . . . .He felt too that she had become invaluable, a woman without equal among a million women, and he could not tell why. (15-16)

The police they have been waiting for come:

> They all went away together, the men walking in a group, María Concepción following a few steps in the rear . . . . No one spoke. (16-17)

The story has a lengthy resolution, the fifth and sixth sections. The danger to María from the police has to be worked out, and Juan says that "there will be something to settle between us afterwards" (15). But there is no suggestion thereafter that an injury to Juan is to be accounted for. The main drift through the resolution is simply a slight rise in suspense and fear (though Juan has promised "thou shalt have nothing to fear") in the scene with the police and, then, final relief.

Other possibilities are implicit as the fifth section begins. We might, for example, expect a further development of Juan's new maturity. But aside from the businesslike account he gives the gendarmes and the bitter realism with which he views his own prospects, there is no marked growth in this direction. Again, some difference on María's side might be expected. The totality of her submission might lead one to think that she has simply reverted to her earlier circumstances and views, and some have, in fact, construed the bleakness of such a return as the basic import of the story.[8]

By killing Rosa, however, María has not simply achieved a primitive justice but has also terminated her childhood, outgrown her pride and isolation as well. The fifth section works out these developments indirectly, especially through unspoken interactions between María and the villagers. The main burden of the last section is to deepen to almost mystical depths her contentment—and to do this in imagery from the natural rhythms of life, particularly of breathing.

At the opening of the fifth section, the combination of wake and inquest is presented heavily in the imagery of restlessness associated with Juan and Rosa. That imagery is now transfixed in the corpse of Rosa, which appears to be still in the agony of death:

> The ridges of the rose-colored rebozo thrown over the body varied continually, as though the thing it covered was not perfectly in repose . . . . The mouth dropped sharply at the corners in a grimace of weeping arrested half-way. The brows were distressed; the dead flesh could not cast off the shape of its last terror. (17)

There is then a set piece for Old Lupe, Rosa's godmother, whose sympathies were earlier seen to have shifted to María Concepción and are now shown to remain with her. Lupe's scene of duping the police has balances in its comic touches with Juan's earlier thwarting of the authorities; it also provides a climax for the superstitious elements of the story.

The recital of their alibi by Juan and María shifts into a summary mode, and these paragraphs (19) appear to restore the serious tone and provide a quieter transition to the peaceful social understanding that concludes the scene and suggests that María has regained not simply contentment but also her place in the community by accepting its help:

> María Concepción suddenly felt herself guarded, surrounded, upborne by her faithful friends. They were around her, speaking for her, defending her, the forces of life were ranged invincibly with her against the beaten dead. María Rosa had thrown away her share of strength in them, she lay forfeited among them. María Concepción looked from one to the other of the circling, intent faces. Their eyes gave back reassurance, understanding, a secret and mighty sympathy. (20)

As the section ends and María claims Rosa's baby as a symbol of her victory, the image of breath provides an appropriate link to the last section:

> "He is mine," she said clearly, "I will take him with me."
> No one assented in words, but an approving nod, a bare breath of complete agreement, stirred among them as they made way for her. (20)

The sixth and final section of the story is divided equally between Juan and María Concepción. It details their physical reaction to their escape and their feelings about their new situation. For Juan, there is simply physical exhaustion. There is also bitterness (a climactic taste image again) about his loss of Rosa and their reckless life with the army and about his prospective return to work and life with María. Juan now feels betrayed by "luck," but it is indeed self-betrayal again. The positive increments to his characterization in the immediately preceding sections are somewhat lowered by these reflections, but there is a leveling off in the realism of "Well, there was no way out of it now" (20). There might even be a slight rise in character assets, in the faint suggestion of accepted suffering in Juan's position in sleep, "his arms flung up and outward" (21), a detail that follows his exclamation, "O Jesus! what bad luck overtakes a man." (20)

For María, on the other hand, there is a new lightness (the theme was introduced in Juan's part of this section: "The occasional light touch of the woman at his elbow . . . " [21]) and a return to the old serenity, now deepened even to ecstasy and enriched with the harmonious response of house and nature. The final paragraph unites these elements of lightness and peace in the natural rhythm of breathing and the bowed drowsing of María.

> María Concepción could hear Juan's breathing. The sound vapored from the low doorway, calmly; the house seemed to be resting after a burdensome day. She breathed, too, very slowly and quietly, each inspiration saturating her with repose. The child's light, faint breath was a mere shadowy moth of sound in the silver air. The night, the earth under her, seemed to swell and recede together with a limitless, unhurried, benign breathing. She dropped and closed her eyes, feeling the slow rise and fall within her own body. She did not know what it was, but it eased her all through. Even as she was falling asleep, head bowed over the child, she was still aware of a strange, wakeful happiness. (21)

María is important to the story, it may finally be said, not simply because she is a convincingly realistic character, a psychologically interesting combination of positive qualities like serenity and industry with the negative values of pride or momentary cruelty. Nor is it simply a quantitative matter, that she is the main character and most of the story is about her. Rather, the character achieves special distinction because it is the functional center of the narrative, because it provides a satisfactory integration of the other parts. It is in the originality of this structuring that it rises above the conventions of the "injured wife" or the "isolated peasant heroine" that we might find in a short story of, say, Maupassant.

In her betrayal and abandonment, María is shown, despite her traumatic reactions, to perdure and to retain her essential self-possession. And when her fortunes are reversed paradoxically by the decisive action of her revenge, she contrasts with the other characters even more clearly and in a way that balances with and reinforces her domination of her own difficulties.[9] Positive eventually dominates negative within María more forcefully than in her original presentation; that same relationship obtains between María and the other characters. She proves more courageous than Juan, more wise than Givens, more passionate than Rosa, more clever than Lupe. As the momentum of her rise in the second part of the story thus gains force (as also through the series of reconciliations with Juan, the villagers, and finally her own self), the lyrical closing of her utter peace achieves an inevitable rightness. It is in this fashion that María's decline and rise provides an appropriate and meaningful function for the largest divisions of the story, that her reactions to the acts of the plot line sustains the rhythm of contentment-betrayal-agony and finally transcends it to end the story.

Within these large patterns, we have only glanced in passing at the much more detailed commerce of balancing and contrasting parts in the narrative. But whether in the structuring of individual scenes and episodes, the management of the different modes of narration, the use of recurrent images adapted to the specific needs of such intermediate structures, or the appropriate variation of smaller stylistic structures in modifying phrases or descriptive details—Porter creates a satisfying coherence which says, nothing need be changed.

Notes

[1] Myron M. Liberman, *Katherine Anne Porter's Fiction* (Detroit: Wayne State University Press, 1971), 7.

[2] Numbers in parentheses refer to pages in Katherine Anne Porter, *The Collected Stories of Katherine Anne Porter* (New York: Harcourt, Brace and World, 1965.)

[3] In what is the most detailed and in some ways the most insightful analysis of imagery and themes in "María Concepción," James Hafley describes walking as an image of order: "Walking is usually towards life; paths (permitting ordered modes of movement) simplify attainment of goals; but running or swerving constitute excesses." (See "María Concepción: Life Among the Ruins," *Four Quarters*, 12 [1962], 12.) Thus, walking with care indicates "that primitive man's own resinous heart furnishes him with modes of conduct essentially like those sanctioned by civilized cultures." One minor difficulty with this interpretation is met to some extent as Hafley modifies his assertion by "usually," for it is indeed difficult to accommodate all instances of walking under the positive significance he suggests. A more pertinent and general objection is that abstracting such series of meanings without further linear analysis does not do sufficient justice to expectations built into the developing text or to relations achieved by balancing and contrasting these meanings with others in specific contexts.

[4]Hafley, 11-12, speaks well to the conflict of civilized and primitive values in the story; see also Darlene Harbour Unrue, *Truth and Vision in Katherine Anne Porter's Fiction* (Athens: The University of Georgia Press, 1985), 16-25.

[5]These are the characteristics of much of Porter's descriptive detail—of the soldier who tells Juan with "impersonal cheerfulness" that he will be executed (10), of the pregnant Rosa received with "professional importance by Lupe" (10), or the officer who saw Juan's "insufferable pantomine" but appeared "to be gazing at a vacuum" (11). Beyond their function in characterization or whatever, such details are sometimes related in a compelling way to other images in the story. There is, for example, the simile of Juan walking "proudly as a gamecock" placed perfectly at the conclusion of his seduction of Rosa but clearly related to the doomed fowl that María binds and butchers for market (3, 7, 12, 13).

[6]William L. Nance, *Katherine Anne Porter and the Art of Rejection* (Chapel Hill: University of North Carolina Press, 1964), 14, describes the style in "María Concepción" as "austere, apparently simple," and he later (pp. 316-17) surveys earlier judgments of Miss Porter's style that feature phrases like "subdued and exceptional brilliance," "subtle and beautiful," "freedom from rarefied mannerisms," simplicities which "are strategems," "a bare art."

[7]Compare Porter's remarks on the posture of the sleeping Mexican man in:*The Collected Essays and Occasional Writing of Katherine Anne Porter* (New York: Delacorte Press, 1970), 389.

> Sometimes he sleeps with his knees drawn up to his chin and his hat over his eyes, forming a kind of pyramid with his blanket round about him. He makes such an attractive design as he sits thus: no wonder people go around painting pictures of him. But I think he sleeps there because he is

numbed with tiredness and has no other place to go, and not in the least because he is a public decoration. Toughened as he may be to hardship, you can never convince me he is really comfortable, or likes this way of sleeping.

[8] See, especially, James W. Johnson, "Another Look at Katherine Anne Porter," *Virginia Quarterly Review* (1960): 610, and the observation of Harry John Mooney, *The Fiction and Criticism of Katherine Anne Porter* (Pittsburgh: University of Pittsburgh, 1957), 49:

So María Concepción returns to the elemental existence of the earth she loves and understands, and the savage primitivism of which she is herself an expression . . . and we are thus brought very close once again to the forces that indicate the "terrible failure of the life of man in the Western World."

But this interpretation contravenes the very positive tone of the closing and suggests a more complicated and pointed thematic development than the story has.

[9] The contrasts with other characters are worked out in many details throughout the story, of course. At the beginning of the third section, for example, Rosa is "burdened" with the child she carries, as opposed to the "free, natural, guarded ease" of María with her unborn child; and Rosa "screaming and falling on her face" as she is dragged to her hut or Juan "limping with foot soreness" (10) contrasts with María's walking. There are similar oppositions in clothing (the presumably simple shirt María could have bought for Juan versus the heavy finery scavenged for him by Rosa), between cleanliness and dirt or silence and garrulity.

William Faulkner: Praise And Learning In The Short Version Of "The Bear"

In the short version of "The Bear," Faulkner used the first section and a half of the longer version and then expanded a brief later episode for a new conclusion. Structured in this fashion, the story deals only with the boy's education, not simply his initiation into the skills of hunting and the virtues of noble hunters, but more especially into a wisdom to be learned only from the forest and from the embodiment of its spirit, the bear Old Ben.

The four opening paragraphs of the story sketch basic contrasts between the boy and the older hunters and between the boy and the bear. What is clear from the beginning is that both the boy and the bear are being presented in the heightened rhetoric of panegyric, and their predestined relationship is treated with "hieratic seriousness."

The rising action has two sequences. In the first, the boy, despite his patient effort, fails to see the bear, though he is certain that Old Ben has studied him. In the second, after abandoning the support of gun, watch, and compass, he succeeds in meeting and exchanging a significant look with the bear, as they "pledged something, affirmed something more lasting." Thereafter, the boy is able to set an ambush but in the climax sacrifices his chance to shoot the bear, ostensibly to save his endangered dog.

In the quiet denouement, his father tries to explain the significance of the climactic moment of forebearance by comparing it to the frozen moment of Keats' Grecian Urn. But the boy, in his own mind, prefers a more simple and personal explanation of what he has learned.

The story, then, successfully combines the detailed realism and drama of the hunting narrative with a symbolic quest for deeper values. It weaves contrasts between man and beast, virgin forest and predatory society, action and stasis and climaxes them in the boy's moment of dangerous communion with the bear in which, paradoxically, his failure as a hunter brings him his most important success as a man.

The short version of Faulkner's story "The Bear" appeared in the *Saturday Evening Post* on May 9, 1942. The more familiar longer version appeared about the same time, as one of seven interrelated stories in *Go Down, Moses*. Until recently, the received opinion was that the short story (together with the story "Lion," published in 1935) was the principal source of the more complex form. It now seems clear, however, that the short story was excerpted from the longer version and carefully rearranged.[1]

There is a third version of the story as well. Faulkner was aware that the longer version depended much for its effect on its context in *Go Down, Moses*. His advice to those reading the story separately was to skip the complex conversation between Isaac and Cass in the long fourth section.[2] And he followed his own advice (as other editors have not) when he printed the longer version in *The Big Woods* in 1955. As Irving Howe pointed out, with that omission "the narrative would flow more easily toward its climax; there would be a more pleasing unity of tone; and the meaning . . . would be allowed to rest in a fine implication . . . pretty much the way Faulkner first printed "The Bear" in its magazine version."[3]

Without considering the relative merits of the versions, one can safely assert that the short (and relatively neglected) version is the most clearly and tightly structured, not simply because of brevity, but also because it deals with a narrower range of thematic elements.[4] It is concerned almost exclusively with the initiation of the boy into the ways and mysteries of the forest and its presiding spirit, the bear Old Ben, and with the skills and virtues needed for that initiation. It deals, that is, with the boy's education. While the short story foreshadows the death of Old Ben and the doom of the forest, it does not get to the tangled relationship of slavery to the exploitation of nature and the sins of forefathers. These are the moral problems which the boy, now become Isaac McCaslin in the longer version, inherits and which he nobly, but rather ineffectually, deals with.

But neither does the success of the short story result from its narrower range as such, but rather, as in every case, from an appropriate balancing and contrasting of whatever elements are used. And here (as in Joyce, though in a quite different mode), we should look to a combination of realistic narrative, a hunting story, with a symbolic quest for more universal values, a combination brought to a suspenseful climax and then unfolded in the quiet instruction of the denouement. What is also important is the sustained and elaborate rhetoric of epideixis, the high praise of Old Ben for his power and primitive mystery and of the boy-hunter for his singular achievement. For what preoccupies the narrator-eulogizer especially is the series of differences and similarities between the boy and the older hunters and between the boy and the bear, as he outdistances their advantages and achieves his wisdom.

The boy begins his initiation at the age of ten by joining his elders on their semiannual hunting trips. What he is to learn, especially from Sam Fathers, "son of a slave woman and a Chickasaw chief," is how to manage in the forest on his own and how to track and kill deer and bear. From his father and his aristocrat friends, he is to learn not simply the hunter's skills as these are reflected in examples of their competence and their talk before the campfire, but also the virtues of endurance and patience, pride in one's ability but humility before the vastness of the forest and the prowess of its denizens. From two dogs, and in different ways, he is to learn courage. With such abilities and, more important, such virtues, he would be worthy to enter the community of adult hunters. But the values Old Ben will finally teach transcend these; they involve a respect for life and for the ageless spirit of the forest itself.

The boy's testing—in isolation from school and family and guided by wiser adults—resembles that of a primitive puberty rite. This is particularly explicit later in the story when he is anointed with the blood of the first buck he kills. The story is also an identity-quest of a young male who seeks to establish his superiority competitively by a heroic deed "that compels recognition from other males."[5] But the boy's initiation is not an ordinary one. As Kenneth La Budde observed many years ago:

> The tests which Ike was submitted to and the instruction which he received from his elders are actually those given to a youth destined for an exalted position among his people. The symbolism of the name *Isaac* is obvious. He had the instinct of his people to a superior degree so that when he went into the woods for the first time he moved instinctively. The scene was something he had always known, for it had been in his very blood.[6]

Very early in the story, therefore, the boy is presented as someone special in his intuitive powers, but, more particularly, as someone set apart from his elders by a special relationship to the fabled bear, Old Ben. His elders, it is made clear, have fallen into a rather passive and detached respect for the bear. Having lost any real hope of a kill, they simply keep a "yearly rendezvous" with the bear, but occupy themselves for the most part in the conviviality of their camp and pro forma runs with hunting dogs. The boy, on the other hand, is from the beginning set actively and single-mindedly toward his meetings with Old Ben and toward the ultimate maturing these meetings will bring him.

As a result, the boy's characterization concentrates on his driving ambition to track down Old Ben. But this drive is tamed and purified by a series of failures and small successes and is gradually transformed as the boy penetrates the mystery of the forest. His initiation differs from that of other young heroes, therefore, in that the climactic episode is not something that befalls him arbitrarily or fatefully, but rather is something that he actively works toward step by step. In the process he himself achieves symbolic dimension as the forest also becomes his teacher. Just as Sam Fathers, the priest of the forest's mysteries, instructs him in the way of wise hunters or his bookish father tries to show him the meaning of his decisive encounter, so the clawed and rotting log in the forest speaks of the return to death in nature's cycles; dogs and mules instruct in different types of fear and courage; Old Ben shows the necessity of risk and renunciation.[7]

By these means and in four short years, the boy exceeds the expectation and even the capability of his human mentors. Several pivotal ironies are thus developed in the story: how the pupil excels his teachers; how apparent enmity of boy and bear becomes a special relationship; how a spiritual understanding can be achieved in that relationship only in increasingly close and physical contact and the actual threat of death; how failure for the hunter brings success in the deeper values of a man. What bridges, then, the episodic and suspenseful developments of the realistic hunting story and the gradually deepening symbolism of a communion with the forest's freedom, innocence, and mysterious permanence, is a pattern which first presents the possibility of this communion, delays its realization, and finally brings it about.

However, in the four lengthy paragraphs of exposition that open the story, the stress is on the gulf between the boy and the bear. The relationship starts as that between a youthful David and a Goliath that haunts his dreams. Thus, starting with the clipped opening sentence, "He was ten," the boy is persistently associated with limited and specific times, whereas the bear moves in the extended and repetitive time of tradition and legend—he "had listened to it for years; the long legend . . . ." Similar contrasts are drawn in size and power; the presumably puny size of the boy is opposed to the "tremendous bear with one trap-ruined foot, which, in an area over almost a hundred miles deep . . ."; between his weakness and that of men generally ("no more effect than so many peas blown through a tube by a boy") and the violent, though not malevolent, power of Old Ben. And the bear's magnitude is expanded even further as he is given dimensions of myth; he was

> not even a mortal animal but an anachronism, indomitable and invincible, out of an old dead time, a phantom, epitome and apotheosis of the old wild life at which the puny humans swarmed and hacked in a fury of abhorrence and fear, like pygmies about the ankles of a drowsing elephant: the old bear solitary, indomitable and alone, widowered, childless, and absolved of mortality—old Priam reft of his old wife and having outlived all his sons (282).

Despite such contrasts and the major emphasis on Old Ben, the boy's special relationship to him is also made clear: he had "inherited the bear," it "ran in his knowledge before he even saw it," it "towered in his dreams." More importantly, he "seemed to see it entire with a child's complete divination before he even laid eyes on" it. His apprehension is natural and intuitive, but also unreflective and even unconscious.

The assertions about the main characters in these first paragraphs are, of course, exaggerated. What is operating is a "principle of enlargement," so a character is "greater than its realistic counterpart in life" and, as "the superlative example of its kind," is intended to be archetypal.[8] That latter result depends upon the whole story. But what establishes some credibility for it immediately is the convincing voice developed for the narrator. Robert Penn Warren described as one of Faulkner's basic narrative methods the organization of episodic structures by the sense of voice: "a narrator's presence (though not necessarily a narrator in the formal sense) is almost constantly felt—a method in which the medium is ultimately a 'voice' as index to sensibility."[9] That orotund and brooding voice is not unfamiliar. But here it is strikingly appropriate to the commemoration and celebration of an important human achievement in a moment elegiacally shaded, at the beginning of the forest's doom. Many of the stylistic features that have been isolated by analysts of Faulkner's writing contribute efficiently to the elevation of style here, as well as to the elaboration of the story's symbolism. If one considers William Van O'Connor's early listing, for example, the long sentences with colons, semi-colons, dashes, and parentheses; the vocabulary that evokes an older morality; the allusions to romantic episodes in history and in literature; the use of synonyms for the purpose of repetition; the piling up of adjectives—all can be said to contribute to the process of amplification necessary for the panegyric. On the other hand, the series of negatives followed by a positive; the poetic extension of the meaning of words; the reaching out for a metaphor or a simile the "vehicle" of which is foreign to the subject being discussed; the use of paradox—all seem to enlarge, to make tentative and complex in a development to a final revelation, the implications of the story.[10] The narrator's rhetoric is not notable for its smaller structures, though there are memorable instances effectively foregrounded in the dense general texture, like the phrase about "the yearly pageant of the old bear's furious immortality." What is more notable is the consistent level of its elevation and comparative clarity (in contrast not simply to Part IV of the longer version, but also to its other sections), the good interplay, nevertheless, with an even shorter and laconic strain, a good management, that is, between several levels of style. Part of the simplification of style would seem to have resulted from the intention to publish the shortened version in a popular magazine, and from the prodding of the *Post* editors who did ask for greater clarity and specifically for a revision of the final paragraph that "would go a long way toward increasing the number of appreciative readers."[11] But what is peculiarly appropriate to the epideictic purpose of prose here are the rolling cadences of southern politician and preacher.[12] And, again, I think it can be argued that beginning with the clipped and dramatic first sentence and the more baroque three paragraphs which follow, there is good contrast between levels of style. This is apparent, too, as the practical style of the fourth paragraph, filled as it is with details of the trips to the camp as the boy observed them, provides an appropriate transition to the main action of the story.

In the middle part of the story (pp. 282-286) the plot structure builds to the first major encounter of boy and bear through two contrastive movements. In the first movement, the boy has a series of failures and delays in his attempts simply to see the bear; in the second, a series of successes that lead to the first sighting. In the first, the young hunter is himself hunted and, in a sense, tantalized by Old Ben. While he does not reveal himself directly to the boy's sight, the bear does allow himself to be progressively sensed in other ways. There is first the "moiling yapping" of the dogs on the trail which the boy hears in the far distance. He then sees indirect but tangible evidence of the bear's presence: the cowering pack, the injured hound, the frightened mule, the footprint by the log. As he looks at the pack under the kitchen floor, he also smells an "Effluvium of something more than dog." Finally, the boy seems to taste the unseen presence of the bear.

The effective climax to this series of incidents is the scene in the bayou. The scene stresses again the boy's separation from his elders; except for Sam, they are on the move with the dogs while he stands in long communion with the forest. The first paragraph given to the scene describes his stand in one long and involved sentence, stressing the solitude and immemorial permanence of the place; the second, in contrasting clipped sentences, suggests the presence of the unseen bear:

> He heard no dogs at all. He never did hear them. He only heard the drumming of the woodpecker stop short off and knew that the bear was looking at him. He never saw it. He did not know whether it was in front of him or behind him. He did not move, holding the useless gun, which he did not cock, tasting in his saliva that taint as of brass which he knew now because he had smelled it when he peered under the kitchen at the huddled dogs. (286)

What this step-by-step awakening of his senses has brought the boy to is the realization that he has been seen completely and that, if he is to have any shred of the hope his elders basically lack, he must in turn see Old Ben.

The second series of incidents in the middle section has the boy in motion. He must leave Sam Fathers, strike out on his own to range further into the forest and learn its ways. His moments of insight, however, continue to be associated with quiet and immobility, his progress with unselfconsciousness: "'It's the gun,' Sam said. He stood beside the fence motionless . . . "(288); "the boy went faster yet still quietly; he was becoming better and better as a woodsman, still without having yet realized it"(288). The element of fear is also expanded as Fathers advises him to be "scared" but not "afraid."

What now emerges more clearly is the pattern of the boy exceeding expectations. Sam had suggested that he leave his gun behind, if he wanted Old Ben to show himself. After his long trek into the forest the next day, he decides also to abandon "the watch, the compass, the stick—the three lifeless mechanicals with which for nine hours he had fended the wilderness off . . . and relinquished completely to it." He is then bereft of external support, with only "that thin, clear, immortal lucidity which alone differed him from this bear," having abrogated "all the old rules and balances of hunter and hunted." He rests quietly and has his vision of the bear "immobile, solid, fixed in the hot dappling of the green and windless noon." What is stressed in this climax is the sympathetic union of the bear and boy: Old Ben "stopped again and looked back at him across one shoulder" (291). As the encounter is recalled later, this sense of union is celebrated more elaborately and related to an earlier time of the forest as an untouched Eden:

> They had looked at each other, they had emerged from the wilderness old as earth, synchronized to the instant by something more than the blood that moved the flesh and bones which bore them, and touched, pledged something, affirmed something more lasting than the frail web of bones and flesh which any accident could obliterate. (291)

And the role of the wilderness and bear as teachers becomes explicit, too—the wilderness is the boy's "college," the bear his "alma mater" (291). But after his appearance, Old Ben fades again mysteriously into the forest and the boy is left with the conviction that the final confrontation will be "next fall."

But his calculation is wrong and the short section (290-292) devoted to the major climax combines features of both failure and success and thus repeats the movements of the middle section. The basic failure, of course, is not to see Old Ben again.

But what proceeds apace is the boy's achievement, still unself-conscious and with some basic elements of unawareness about his situation. For example, his area of competence in the forest, thirty miles, moves into the range of Old Ben's domination of a hundred miles. With his ritual anointing with the buck's blood and his increased familiarity with the bear's patterns of travel, his worthiness for another sighting is re-established. The final encounter, however, will be possible only after two realizations—that in their first exchange of looking they had pledged something (though this is not fully understood) and the belatedly recalled advice of Sam that the "right" dog will be needed to hold the bear at bay. The dog in question is a clear analogue of the boy—small, humble, but "possessing that bravery which had since stopped being courage and had become foolhardiness."

In the final encounter, it is not simply pity for the fyce but rather the pledge of reverence for Old Ben and what he represented in the forest that makes it impossible for the boy to shoot, that leads him to sacrifice victory to life. Despite the presence of Sam and the dogs, the boy is said to be alone, and it is in this aloneness that his special identification with the bear appears most clearly. With a mixture of terror and love, violence and stillness,

> He could smell it, strong and hot and rank. Sprawling, he looked up to where it loomed and towered over him like a cloudburst and colored like a thunderclap, quite familiar, peacefully and even lucidly familiar, until he remembered: This was the way he had used to dream about it. Then it was gone. (292)

It is a brief moment, but it is sharply etched and full of shade and light. It comes at the end of a long series of contrasting episodes involving the boy's dreams and imaginings, the indefiniteness and elusiveness of the bear, the dark gloom of the forest into which he fades. It is also a moment of frozen time, as many commentators have observed, with transcendental, not to say mystical, overtones.[13] Its explication becomes the burden of the extended denouement.

This final section (292-295), which opens dramatically in the middle of a dialogue, which has much of the classroom about it, is also divided into two movements of about equal length. In the first, the father attempts to explain the boy's experience to him in terms of Keat's "Grecian Urn".[14] Since the young hunter has declined to destroy life of special significance, the embodiment of the forest's meaning, he has understood it. More specifically, he has had a moment of ideal relationship in which, like the Urn figures, he has aspired to pure freedom and, in some sense, attained it; a moment revealing the primeval spirit of the forest, to which he can continue to return; a permanent moment embodying the highest human values held by the heart.

In the second part, the boy rejects this explanation of his experience through a literary example in favor of his own simple and intuitive apprehension and the concrete example of "Sam, and Old Ben, and Nip." What is of prime importance is the humility and pride of Sam, who led him to the experience; the courage of the fyce that showed him how to combine those apparently contradictory qualities of humility and pride; the forebearance of both the boy and Old Ben which preserved the moment as one of special insight and wisdom. And there is finally the approval of a bookish, loving father:

> Sam, and Old Ben, and Nip, he thought. And himself too. He had been all right too. His father had said so. "Yes, sir," he said.(295)

In the final instance, again, the boy exceeds expectations—his father's, about how he understands his experience; his own, for there is no longer any possibility of mistake or uncertainty. It is in peaceful assurance and clear consciousness that he accepts himself, that he can combine humility and pride.

What is particularly successful in the story's structure, again, is the detailed and finished combination of the realistic hunting narrative with the symbolic initiation into deep mysteries, what Eudora Welty describes as "alternately dilating reality to the reach of abstraction and bringing it home with a footprint." That combination is developed through a simple pattern of suggestion, delay, and realization, through a series of ironies about the boy, and through several basic contrasts—particularly of man and beast, forest and society, hunter and quarry, action and stasis—oppositions which switch places at times and begin to interpenetrate until they climax in the boy's communion with the bear.[15] The most important irony is the way the boy exceeds expectation, most particularly in the climax where his failure as a hunter brings him his most important success as a man. Furthermore, the pattern of expectations exceeded is the basic material of the narrator's panegyric, the achievement of the boy for which the rhetorical structure elicits our admiration. This structure is developed with such consistency of tone, such effective management of involved syntactic figures, as well as of general levels of style, that the final relationships are strikingly appropriate—and they themselves become the literary structure of an exceptional story.

Notes

[1] See Joseph Blotner, *Faulkner: A Biography* (New York: Random House, 1974) II, 1088; James Early, *The Making of Go Down, Moses*

(Dallas: Southern Methodist University Press, 1972), 22-39; Edward M. Holmes, *Faulkner's Twice-Told Tales* (The Hague: Mouton, 1966), 68-71; Hans Skei, *William Faulkner: the Short Story Career* (Oslo: Universitet-forlaget, 1981), 88, 97.

[2] Frederick L. Gwynn and Joseph Blotner, eds., *Faulkner at the University* (Charlottesville: University of Virginia Press, 1959), 273.

[3] Irving Howe, *William Faulkner: A Critical Study* (New York: Random House, 1962), 257.

[4] The story was reprinted in Francis Lee Utley, Lynn Y. Bloom, and Arthur K. Kinney, eds., *Bear, Man, and God: Seven Approaches to William Faulkner's The Bear* (New York: Random House, 1964); it was, however, dropped in the second edition (1971). It also appeared in Martha Foley, ed., *The Best American Short Stories* (Boston: Houghton Mifflin, 1943); its appearance in Joseph Blotner, ed., *Uncollected Stories of William Faulkner* (New York: Random House, 1979), 281-95, constitutes a belated standard edition to which page numbers in parentheses here refer.

[5] Victor Strandberg, "Between Truth and Fact: Faulkner's Symbols of Identity", *Modern Fiction Studies* 21 (1975): 450; see also Robert Harrison, "Faulkner's 'The Bear': Some Notes on Form," *Georgia Review* 20 (1966): 318-20.

[6] "Cultural Primitivism in William Faulkner's 'The Bear,'" *American Quarterly* 2 (1950): 326.

[7] Walter Davis remarks that everything "connected with the wilderness exists, as it were, for the formation of Ike's character. . . . Because Faulkner so clearly underscores the educational significance of the wilderness for the formation and testing of human character, we desire Ike's "novitiate" to it for the sake of his own moral growth. Faulkner maximizes that response by describing Ike's initiation in terms strongly reminiscent of 'the myth of the birth of the hero' . . . as

a means of narrative magnification in order to invest Ike's development with ethical significance," *The Act of Interpretation* (Chicago: University of Chicago Press, 1978), 16. Thomas Merton, while he does not see the religious elements as specifically Christian, also speaks of the first episodes of "The Bear" as "the story of a disciple being taught and formed in a traditional and archaic wisdom by a charismatic spiritual Father who is especially qualified for the task and who hands on not only a set of skills or a body of knowledge, but a *mastery of life*, a certain way of being aware, of being in touch with not just living things, but with the cosmic spirit, with the wilderness itself regarded almost as a supernatural being, a 'person.' Indeed, the Bear, Old Ben, is treated as a quasi-transcendent being . . . " "'Baptism in the Forest': Wisdom and Initiation in William Faulkner," in George Panichas, ed., *Mansions of the Spirit* (New York: Hawthorn Books, 1967), 30.

[8] Stanley L. Elkin, "Religious Themes and Symbolism in the Novels of William Faulkner," (Dissertation, University of Illinois, 1961), 275.

[9] Robert Penn Warren, "William Faulkner," in *William Faulkner: Two Decades of Criticism*, ed., Frederick J. Hoffman and Olga W. Vickery (East Lansing: Michigan State University Press, 1951), 99.

[10] William Van O'Connor, "Rhetoric in Southern Writing: Faulkner," *Georgia Review* 12 (Spring 1958): 83-86; reprinted in *Bear, Man and God*, 293-296. For relevant features of Faulkner's style see also Walter J. Slatoff, "The Pattern of Faulkner's Rhetoric," *Twentieth Century Literature* 3 (1957): 107-27; James L. Radomski, "Faulkner's Style: a Syntactic Analysis," *Dissertation Abstracts International* 35 (1975): 6154A; and Gail L. Montimen, "Rhetoric of Loss: An Analysis of Faulkner's Perceptual Style," *DAI* 37 (1976): 971A-72A.

[11] See Blotner, 1088.

[12] See Helen Swink, "William Faulkner: The Novelist as Oral Narrator," *Georgia Review* 26 (1972): 183-209, but more especially,

Carl F. Hovde, "Faulkner's Democratic Rhetoric", *South Atlantic Quarterly* 63 (1964): 530-41, for interesting suggestions about the genesis of Faulkner's high style.

[13] See, for example, Karl E. Zink, "Flux and the Frozen Moment," *PMLA* 71 (1956): 285-301, and Lynn Altenbrand, "A Suspended Moment: The Irony of History in William Faulkner's 'The Bear,'" *Modern Language Notes* 75 (1960): 579.

[14] For commentary, see Blanche Gelfant, "Faulkner and Keats: The Ideality of Art in 'The Bear,'" *Southern Literary Journal* 2 (1969): 43-65; William Stone, "Ike McCaslin and the Grecian Urn," *Studies in Short Fiction* 10 (1973): 93-94; Joan Korenman, "Faulkner's Grecian Ode," *Southern Literary Journal* 7 (1974): 3-23.

[15] See Dirk Kuyk, Jr., *Threads Cable-Strong: William Faulkner's* **Go Down, Moses** (Lewisburg: Bucknell University Press, 1983), 106-110.

Ernest Hemingway: Nick's "Big Two-Hearted River"

Hemingway's "Big Two-Hearted River" is really a brace of stories about a solitary fishing trip which a young man takes to escape the mounting pressures of his life. Both parts are loosely structured in three sections, each section presenting much detail about the difficulties and pleasures, but more especially about the methodically performed tasks, of the sportsman on the first two days of his trip.

The first part emphasizes Nick's growing satisfaction despite the exertions of the first day and his profound happiness in the camp he finally arranges. The second part starts on a high pitch of contentment, declines a bit after some bad luck in fishing, and ends ambiguously with the threatening challenge of the swamp that Nick decides not to fish that day.

What is centrally developed in both parts, however, is the special relationship of sportsman and nature. At first, nature is primarily a background which Nick gauges in a way that defines his own position, a wasteland out of which he toils toward a campsite until, through an increas-

ingly benevolent ambience, he reaches his "good place." In the second part, there is a more energetic interaction of man and nature, underlined by increasingly animistic imagery, a give and take with grasshoppers trapped for bait, the river and its currents, the trout caught and lost, the dark swamp. And the basic rhythm of this interaction is set from the beginning in a repeated sequence in which Nick sees a part of nature in precise detail, does what is appropriate or necessary in the situation, and reacts with satisfaction to what he sees and does.

Hemingway's "Big Two-Hearted River" describes some twenty-four hours of a writer's solitary fishing trip in northern Michigan. The first part has Nick Adams arriving at the burnt-out town of Seney; his arduous hike to a campsite; his precise arrangement of the camp and his satisfying first meal there. In the second part, we are told of his equally methodic preparations for trout fishing the next morning; the specific incidents of his fishing; finally, his concluding tasks and return to camp.

However, these narrative facts, and their arrangement in a balanced tripartite pattern, are presented in what Allen Tate called "the most completely realized naturalistic fiction of the age," and in a style John Updike described as "blunt yet somehow urgent and luminous." In recent years, other critics have emphasized that, with the bare and unadorned reality of this story, there comes a weight of significant, ultimately symbolic, implication that makes it a masterpiece.[1]

We easily infer, for example, from Nick's memories of earlier trips with friends, that he is alone now because he wants to be or, more likely, because he has to be. He is meeting some needs which he mentions directly—"the need for thinking, the need to write, other needs" (210).[2] Among the "other needs," there may be something more painful—the necessity to escape the memories of war, his own wounding, the fear of life's meaninglessness or nada—painful experiences which the context of other Nick Adams' stories can readily supply. These latter possibilities are indeed the basis for most current interpretations of the story.[3] Hence, the fishing trip and Nick's immersion in the step-by-step routines of outdoor life are primarily considered protections against these ugly memories; they are defenses against nervous collapse, rituals of redemption in the wasteland of our time.

The problem with such interpretations, however, is that they tend to sacrifice the autonomy of the story, squeezing it into a biography of Nick Adams which has been patched together from other stories; that they ignore Nick's ability to laugh off difficulties in the story and so translate its positive tone into one large irony; that they oversymbolize Nick's deliberateness, when simpler explanations are at hand in Hemingway's code. I will argue here, therefore, that "Big Two-Hearted River" is a story of healing, not of sickness, of general satisfaction, not of constant fear; that, against that dominant ground, symbols of burnt land or swamp should be interpreted as subordinate elements; and that the very satisfying literary structure of the story most centrally involves Nick's special relation to nature as sportsman not mystic.

As the narrative opens, Nick arrives by train at Seney, expecting to find a normal, small town, perhaps a stop-over before hiking to his campsite. But now he sits to view the desolation of a town destroyed by a forest fire. If the destruction is meant to reflect his own condition or the situation of a world that had been ravaged by war, that is not made explicit. Rather the fact that "there was no town" is contrasted immediately with the fact that "the river was there." And it is alive with trout, poised symbolically against the force of the current and darting off to new positions as Nick observes them:

> The river was there. It swirled against the log piles of the bridge. Nick looked down into the clear, brown water, colored from the pebbly bottom, and *watched* the trout keeping themselves steady in the current with wavering fins. As he *watched* them they changed their positions by quick angles, only to hold steady in the fast water again. Nick *watched* them a long time.
>
> He *watched* them holding themselves with their noses into the current, many trout in deep, fast moving water, slightly distorted as he *watched* far down through the glassy convex surface of the pool, its surface pushing and swelling smooth against the resistance of the log-driven piles of the bridge. At the bottom of the pool were the big trout. Nick *did not see* them at first. Then he *saw* them at the bottom of the pool, big trout looking to hold themselves on the gravel bottom in a varying mist of gravel and sand, raised in spurts by the current.
>
> Nick *looked* down into the pool from the bridge. It was a hot day. A kingfisher flew up the stream. It was a long time since Nick *had looked* into a stream *and seen* trout. *They were very satisfactory*. (209-10; emphasis added)

The passage indicates that Hemingway's lean style also has its frequent and rhythmic repetitions, the verbs of seeing emphasized here, but also the prepositions that pinpoint the objects of Nick's observations and, in turn, specify the position of the observer. Thus, Nick is seen standing on the bridge and scanning the river beneath him, then later turning to observe features of the river downstream. At the beginning of the story, he sits on his baggage presumably noting, in one direction, the train going "on up the track out of sight, around one of the hills of burnt timber" and, in the other direction, the layout of the town that was not there. Care is being taken, then, to establish the coordinates of the observer's position, the physical relation of man and nature. But, in a final step, the psychological relation also becomes important: after the report of intense and detailed observation, there is the simple statement that Nick finds the trout "very satisfactory." After further observation of a trout breaking water and tightening its position to face the current, the pitch of the reaction is raised a bit: "Nick's heart tightened. . . . He felt all the old feeling."

The understatement leaves to vaguer implication the precise nature and range of feeling here, presumably the response of sportsman to the lure of his prey or, perhaps, to its natural beauty, but also to its symbolic freedom and its strength. And the larger contrast of wasted and vital nature, of burnt land and animated river, also implies that what nature can offer Nick in its emptiness and fullness, stillness and motion, burnt-blackness and light, is not simply escape and a renewed peace to be enjoyed but also challenge and possible failure to be confronted. Nevertheless, compared to their vividly described occasions, Nick's reactions in the whole story are relatively simple—a minimized emotion or implied judgment, a moment of disappointment, perhaps, of wary caution or suppressed fear. But, typically, the reaction is one of satisfaction and happiness. Even with Hemingway's usual restraint in describing the interior life of a character, the reactions here come with notable regularity.

The progression through the relatively simple incidents of the story is, therefore, rather complicated. The sequence is chronological, the essentially natural development of any account of a fishing trip. But there is an obvious interest in accumulating detail in two distinct ways—in observing the particulars of a scene with some precision or, as will soon develop, in performing the usual chores of a woodsman or fisherman with methodic care. Then, typically, Nick reflects on or, in briefer emotional flashes, reacts to what he sees or does. In this fashion, the sequence of *seeing, doing,* and, more briefly, *reacting* becomes the basic recurrence of the story's structure, the basic, recurring step in Nick's developing relationship with nature.

What seems to be established first in the story, however, is simply nature as a setting for human action, that is, for Nick's labor and rest, waking and sleeping, hungering and eating. Against this background, Nick will go beyond the normal challenges of a camping situation to test himself. He will carry a pack that is "much too heavy," he will go "as far upstream as he could go in one day's walking," he will endure his hunger until he has set up camp. The first instance might suggest that the trip is being used simply to test physical prowess. But, as one expects with Hemingway's heroes, there is also an assertion of human identity in control over disorganization, in resourcefulness, and, above all in this story, in the skilled techniques necessary for survival.

There are self-imposed challenges, therefore, but also the requirements of doing something the *proper* way:

> He adjusted the pack harness around the bundle, pulling straps tight, slung the pack on his back, got his arms through the shoulder straps and took some of the pull off his shoulders by leaning his forehead

against the wide band of the tump-line. Still, it was too heavy. It was much too heavy. He had his leather rod-case in his hand and leaning forward to keep the weight of the pack high on his shoulders he walked along the road that paralleled the railway track, leaving the burned town behind in the heat, and then turned off around a hill with a high, fire-scarred hill on either side onto a road that went back into the country. He walked along the road feeling the ache from the pull of the heavy pack. The road climbed steadily. It was hard work walking up-hill. His muscles ached and the day was hot, but Nick felt happy. (210)

Satisfaction, then, results at least in part from having tested oneself to the limit and from having followed the prescriptions set by experienced teachers—much as the sporting victory over a big trout involves the limited weight of the line used against it, as well as the skills which the good fisherman has learned.[4]

Nick's hike to his campsite is, thus, undertaken with definite standards and restrictions. His walk leads him through three stages of the terrain—out of the dead, fire-blackened hills, through the living plain of sweet fern and pine, to the high ground and meadow by the river. Early in the trip a rhythm of labor and rest is begun. After climbing the steep road through the blackened hills, Nick sits down against a charred stump and smokes a cigarette:

> As he smoked, his legs stretched out in front of him, he noticed a grasshopper walk along the ground and up onto his woolen sock. The grasshopper was black. As he walked along the road, climbing, he had started many grasshoppers from the dust. They were all black. They were not the big grasshoppers with yellow and

> black or red and black wings whirring out from their
> black wing sheathing as they fly up. These were just
> ordinary hoppers, but all a sooty black in color. Nick
> had wondered about them as he walked, without really
> thinking about them. Now, as he watched the black
> hopper that was nibbling at the wool of his sock with
> its fourway lip, he realized that they had all turned
> black from living in the burned-over land. He realized
> that the fire must have come the year before, but the
> grasshoppers were all black now. He wondered how
> long they would stay that way. (211-212)

After examining the grasshopper and concluding that it has been completely blackened by its environment, Nick releases it: "Go on, hopper. . . . Fly away somewhere" (212). The implied reaction here, as it was to the wasteland itself ("The river was there. . . . It could not all be burned") is at least realistic, if not positive and affirmative. While the grasshopper may, perhaps, be a victim of man's carelessness or even, like Nick, represent the ravages of war, it has adapted to the effects of disaster—and it should be freed to continue the struggle.

The contrast between human labor and rest is repeated in the next stretch of backpacking, but now in a setting of living nature, of "heathery sweet fern" and "big islands of pine." Nick finds shaded rest in one such island, after the growth and conjunction of the pines is described in detail:

> Nick slipped off his pack and lay down in the shade.
> He lay on his back and looked up into the pine trees.
> His neck and back and the small of his back rested as
> he stretched. The earth felt good against his back. He
> looked up at the sky, through the branches, and then
> shut his eyes. He opened them and looked up again.

There was a wind high up in the branches. He shut his eyes again and went to sleep. (213)

As evening approaches, Nick awakens and labors forward a third time, but more briefly. Like Eliot's Magi after their trying journey, Nick comes down a hillside to a meadow and at "the edge of the meadow flowed the river." He has found the place—and his paradoxical and understated reaction after he had settled in, is that

He could have made camp hours before if he wanted to. There were plenty of good places to camp on the river. But this was good. (216)

The third section of the story, after Nick's arrival, is more complex. There are first the detailed tasks of a camper and fisherman setting up camp: levelling ground, erecting the tent, securing supplies in a tree, cooking supper. Supper itself is then a special occasion and, finally, Nick prepares his coffee, remembering his friend Hopkins' method. In the process, Nick has his major and most elaborate reaction to something at hand and the longest of his excursions into memory.

As Nick prepares the ground for his tent, what is emphasized is that he has found a level place and is intent on making it even smoother, after the ups and downs of his journey through burnt hills and hollows and the uneven pine plain. When, after much chopping wood, driving pegs, stretching canvas "drum tight" he enters the tent, his reaction is somewhat confused, but the depth of his satisfaction is clear:

Inside the tent the light came through the brown canvas. It smelled pleasantly of canvas. Already there was something mysterious and homelike. Nick was happy as he crawled inside the tent. He had not been unhappy all day. This was different though. Now things were done. There had been this to do. Now it was done. It had been a hard trip. He was very tired. That was done. He had made his camp. He was settled. Nothing could touch him. It was a good place to camp. He was there, in the good place. He was in his home where he had made it. Now he was hungry. (215)

While there may be ritual overtones in the preparation and eating of his supper that Nick then proceeds to, these seem to overlay the more basic notions of care and competence in all his procedures.5 More definite is the reaction of deep satisfaction again, as he takes his first bite while he surveys his camp and, in a mix of thanksgiving and simple macho, exclaims "Chrise . . . Geezus Chrise."

There is new emphasis in this final section on water—the river itself, dew, the bucket of water taken from the river to brew the coffee, "the coffee according to Hopkins." In part, this motif continues the religious suggestions, in part it repeats the more general association of water with life and renewal. On the other hand, the memories of Hopkins (developed in somewhat of a jumble) are, like his coffee, finally bitter: the promised reunion of friends never materialized. This extended episode of memory is not interpreted. Presumably, we are to take the ironic outcome, at which Nick is able to laugh, as a commentary on more general failures of society to meet one's "needs." Nick might have been with other fishermen now or even close friends; the implication is that he would not have had the support and satisfaction he has found from nature in his solitary escape.

Nick's final satisfaction is to go to sleep after his day of labor, curled up in the security of his tent, a clean, well-levelled place.

He has come to his good place by train, road, pathless field and wood, but most of all by his careful observation, his sense of direction, and his competence as woodsman.

Part II of the story is also loosely structured into three main sections: Nick's preparations for his first day of fishing, the incidents of the fishing itself, and its aftermath. However, while the first Part emphasized Nick's growing satisfaction and his ultimate happiness in his camp despite the difficulties and exertions of the day, the second Part starts on a high pitch of happiness, declines with some bad luck in fishing, and ends somewhat ambiguously with the threatening challenge of the swamp. The relation, then, between the dominant and subordinate affective elements of the first story are now readjusted, if not reversed. This difference may relate to the title: the river (and its country) is big but two-hearted in the proportionate satisfaction and disappointment it has to offer.

The first section of Part II (the first thirteen paragraphs) details Nick's preparations. There is an introductory scene, however, with a rather Eden-like aura, as Adams crawls out of his tent and, half-dressed, surveys his sunlit and dewy landscape. A key phrase is echoed from the beginning of Part I: "There was the meadow, the river and the swamp." The phrasing also has a touch of poetic metonymy ("Nick crawled out . . . to look at the morning") and, with heavy stresses on the third syllable, some careful cadencing ("There were birch trees / in the green / of the swamp / on the other side / of the river"). In the second paragraph, the specific detail of the scene is continued and is followed by Nick's explicit reaction: "Nick was excited. He was excited by the early morning and the river" (221).

The tripartite patterning continues in Nick's preparations for the day: readying food for his breakfast and lunch, gathering bait, assembling his fishing gear. The bait is grasshoppers, now healthy and thriving, though conveniently slowed by the morning dew in the meadow. By contrast with the blackened victims of Part I, the abundant grasshoppers here seem to function in the balance of nature as a ready, almost cooperative, sacrifice to the trout.

After he gathers a bottle full of them, Nick returns to his camp fire to make three buckwheat cakes, eat two of them, and save one which, together with two onion sandwiches, he wraps for his lunch. He then prepares his rod, leaders, and hooks—and with a net and bag for his catches—proceeds to the water, feeling "awkward and professionally happy with all his equipment hanging from him" (223).

What is stressed as Nick enters the water is the intimate exchange between nature and man (and even Nick's clothing)—but an exchange which is not without unpleasantness to be coped with:

> He stepped into the stream. It was a shock. His trousers clung tight to his legs. His shoes felt the gravel. The water was a rising cold shock.
>
> Rushing, the current sucked against his legs. Where he stepped in, the water was over his knees. He waded with the current. The gravel slid under his shoes. He looked down at the swirl of water below each leg and tipped up the bottle to get a grasshopper. (224)

Similarly, the day's fishing will have its positive and negative aspects. At first, losses will dominate—a small trout which Nick drops back, taking care not to injure it further (as he remembers the careless habits of other fishermen) and then a huge trout which after a strong fight breaks the leader. Nick's reaction to the loss is the most directly intense of the story, a complex of painful excitement, keen disappointment, vague queasiness, and large admiration: "By God, he was a big one. By God, he was the biggest one I ever heard of" (227). Because he "did not want to rush his sensations any," Nick climbs out of the river to the edge of the meadow, smokes a cigarette, laughs at a tiny trout that rises to his match, lets his disappointment drain out of him.

Moving to a third spot in the river, Nick returns to the contest. He has two catches, losing a third trout in between as he shifts his position twice again. Each try is described in detail. But Nick's reactions get minimal attention until he considers the possibility of fishing the deep waters of the swamp. With some thought about its difficulties and a strong suggestion of fear (associations, perhaps, with other locales of danger), he concludes that "the fishing would be tragic" in this swamp.

But these reflections and emotional reactions come after Nick has climbed a big log to lunch and smoke in the shade. Presumably this is a midday break and more fishing is to follow. But as Nick considers the swamp, his plans apparently change. He is content to kill and clean his two trout (there is a compensating overlay of male imagery in this scene) and to return to the security of his camp.

The story concludes with his notion that "there were plenty of days coming when he could fish the swamp." The ending is ambiguous: possibly a failure of nerve, more likely a prudent decision to back off for a while, not unlike the rests of the previous day, but with the intention of returning to the challenge. Nick knows his limits, even as he continues to test them.

The literary structure of "Big Two-Hearted River" has some of the normal, the expected kinds of unity of any good story and, of course, its unique relationships as well. There are, first, the consistencies of the narration itself which, for example, keeps to a narrow range of perspective between that of the objective and impersonal narrator and of the hero himself. The slightly didactic tone of the narrator is maintained successfully, too, as the "proper" methods of woodsman and fisherman are demonstrated in the story. To some extent the tone is a carry-over from the earlier newspaper accounts Hemingway was using as material for the story.[6] Fortunately, it is more subdued here, but skillfully supported by an occasional technical term: the *spiles* of the bridge, the *tump-line* of the backpack, a *swale* of fern, the *snell* of the hook, a *marly* stream, the *vent* and *milt* of trout.

It can be argued, too, that typical features of Hemingway's simplified style—the clipped sentence with active verb, basic vocabulary with minimal modification, the frequent parataxis with *and* that reduces analytical relations, the reticence about emotion—are unusually appropriate to this outdoor story, with the central character attempting to escape the various complexities of his life for the presumably simpler life of nature.

But the most basic and interesting pattern, as I have suggested, is the more complex relation of the hero to the natural setting. This relationship is developed in the story as something exclusive and optimal, one open only to the skilled outdoorsman who is faithful to a general code and to the detailed models he has for the tasks of his sport. The satisfactions of such a relationship are achieved here in more than generous measure, though not without their realistic limit and contrast. While the story, then, may suggest that Nick has a troubled psychohistory, that wasteland and swamp involve the terrors of *nada*, or that the supper and immersion in the river have religious overtones, the sustained and major emphasis of the story seems to be on the Hemingway code as such, on ethical and aesthetic value achieved in an interaction with nature by expertise, courage, "grace under pressure."

I have suggested that the special relation which results is achieved in the story by a frequently repeated sequence: Nick *sees* the reality of nature as it is, he *does* what is appropriate or necessary in the situation, he *reacts* with satisfaction to what he has seen or done. In "traumatic" interpretations of the story, again, Nick's obsessive care in step-by-step procedures (his observations are usually ignored) are taken as defensive maneuvers against nervous instability or against "the need for thinking." But the same features, as I have argued here, can be related to the expert's need to do something the "right" way, and they are also clearly a source of the story's impressive vividness and immediacy.

We have seen that Nick's reactions, on the other hand, are reported without much detail, in general and understated terms, whether in a brief reflection, a memory stirred by the occasion, an off-handed judgment of what has been observed, a clearly affective response or the implication of some feeling like relief. But in the following sequence from the opening scene (210), for example:

> He turned and looked down the stream. It stretched away, pebbly-bottomed with shallows and big boulders and a deep pool as it curved away around the foot of a bluff.
>
> Nick walked back up the ties to where his pack lay in the cinders beside the railway track. He was happy.

I do not mean to suggest that what is seen or done produces the specific effect. Rather, the reactions seem to be expressions of a relatively stable feeling which Nick has from "the time he had gotten down off the train." Thus, the observations and actions in this natural setting simply evoke a basic feeling, reiterate, and reinforce it.[7]

Again, the interaction of man and nature has mixed value. Man can abuse nature: the fishermen who handle the trout carelessly, someone who may have negligently caused the forest fire, Nick himself, were he not catching grasshoppers at the best time of day. Nature can be difficult, too. Trout may be too small to keep or too big to land, hills can be steep, swamps can be tangled and treacherous. Nick may delight in the morning scene, but he must also secure his supplies against predators, endure the heat of the sun or the bother of mosquitos.

Nevertheless, the positive relation of man to nature is developed consistently in the story as something close and special, perhaps most subtly by the pervasively animistic coloring Hemingway gives to his language. He uses, that is, a variety of personifications, metonymies, and metaphors that give human qualities to animal or vegetable, animate qualities to inanimate elements and even, occasionally, reverses these processes.

There are, for example, a few "dead" metaphors—the "foot" of a bluff, the "brow" of a hill, the "open mouth" of a tent, the four "legs" of a grill and even a few suggestions of animal movement in Nick as he "crawls" or "wallows." But much more frequent are the faint touches of personification in nature or of animation in materials connected with man. In Part I, for example, the train "went on up," saloons "left not a trace," the river is "pushing," trout hold themselves "with their nose into the current," a big trout "lost his shadow," the road "climbed steadily . . . ran on . . . reached the top," Nick knows where he wants to "strike" or "hit" the river, branches of pine trees "interlock," there are "jackpines" and "flapjacks," the canvas bucket "bellied and pulled hard in the current," Nick "tucked" chips under the grill.

In Part II, the log shelter of the grasshoppers is a "lodging house," grease slides across the frying pan "spitting sharply," Nick is careful not to let the hook "bite into his finger," a grasshopper pokes "its face out of the bottle," takes hold of the hook and spits on it, the small trout is "tired," the big trout is "angry."

There are odder expressions, sometimes ellipses, that suggest transfers of animate and inanimate: a trout leaps and "catches the sun," underfoot "the ground was good walking," there are "islands of pines," Nick "did not want anything making lumps under his blanket," the sack "flapped against his legs," the breast pockets with his lunch "bulged against him," the current "sucked against his legs," his trousers "clung tight to his legs," his shoes "felt the gravel," the log was "gray to the touch," he was sure "he would get hooked in the branches," the fishing rod is "jointed" and, when a trout strikes, it comes "alive."

As standard and unavoidable as many of these expressions may be in everyday language,[8] their frequency here serves to bring the country alive. While their faintness and generality harmonize well with other restraints of the story, their consistent use enlarges and heightens the intimate exchange of man and nature. In the context they provide, even Nick's spoken words to the grasshopper he sets free or to nature in general as he rationalizes his use of canned goods, fall into place with some reduction of their possible sentimentality.

Some related motifs in the diction support the basic animism. In particular, there is much movement—large scale motion up and down, in and out, angular and circular; the smaller scale, successive motion of the detailed procedures; the psychological movement of forgetting and remembering. Similarly, there are notable images of escape (and by contrast, of confinement). And the intense dynamism relates also, of course, to

Hemingway's verb-conscious style and his staccato sentence structure.[9] In another feature, the animism of the basic relationship is made more sensitive by images of touch, taste, and smell: sweet heathery fern, floors of pine needles, the delicate skin of trout—but most frequently and simply, of course, by the *water* that relates many of these motifs.

Something can also be said for the tight focus of the story as a source of its satisfying unity.[10] Stories like "Cat in the Rain" and "Hills Like White Elephants" have been praised for the force and economy of their oblique presentations. "Big Two-Hearted River" is much longer and more detailed, but it achieves those same qualities by reducing the agents of the narrative essentially to two, the man and his natural setting, making the basic action the relationship developing between the two, and having that relationship function centrally in the thematic structure. The natural settings in which his characters act out their dramas, says Wright Morris, are not used as in Hardy "to dwarf man to insignificance; rather they remind him in the complex way Hemingway will not permit his characters, of the paradise lost that might still be regained."[11]

"Big Two-Hearted River" is indeed as much about "country" as about Nick. In the long coda which Hemingway fortunately dropped from the story, a stream-of-consciousness about his writing career, Nick says that "he wanted to write about country so it would be here like Cezanne had done it in painting. . . . Nobody had ever written about country like that. . . . You could do it if you would fight it out. If you'd lived right with your eyes."[12] Hemingway wrote to Gertrude Stein soon after he had finished the story and remarked jauntily that it was long, that "nothing happens and the country is swell, I made it all up, so I see it all and part of it comes out the way it ought to."[13] It was indeed swell, and it was Nick's country that came out as it ought to.

Notes

[1] Symbolic reading, especially of Nick-as-Sick, began in earnest with Malcolm Cowley; see especially his introduction to *The Portable Hemingway* (New York: Viking Press, 1945). Among earlier revisionist critics of this emphasis, see E.M. Holliday, "Hemingway's Ambiguity: Symbolism and Irony," *American Literature* 28 (1956): 1-22, and Chaman Nahal, *The Narrative Pattern in Hemingway's Fiction*, (Rutherford: Fairleigh Dickinson University Press, 1971), 101-08.

[2] Page references in parentheses are to the text of "Big Two-Hearted River" in *The Short Stories of Ernest Hemingway* (New York: Scribner's, 1963).

[3] See, in particular, Philip Young, *Ernest Hemingway: A Reconsideration* (University Park: Pennsylvania State University Press, 1966), 30-31. Most extended analyses of the story—earlier ones are listed conveniently in the helpful collection of criticism edited by Jackson J. Benson, *The Short Stories of Ernest Hemingway* (Durham: Duke University Press, 1975), 335-36—follow this approach. Among the more important, see William Adair, "Landscapes of the Mind," *College Literature* 4 (1977): 144-51; Paul Anderson, "Nick's Story in Hemingway's 'Big Two-Hearted River,'" *Studies in Short Fiction* 7 (1970): 564-72; Carlos Baker, *Hemingway: The Writer as Artist* (Princeton: Princeton University Press, 1956), 125-28; Jackson J. Benson, *Hemingway: The Writer's Art of Self Defense* (Minneapolis: University of Minnesota Press, 1969), 137-40; Robert Gibb, "He Made Him Up: 'Big Two-Hearted River' as *Doppelganger*," *Hemingway Notes* 5 (1975): 20-24; James L. Green, "Symbolic Sentences in 'Big Two-Hearted River,'" *Modern Fiction Studies* 14 (1968): 307-12; Shelden N. Grebstein, *Hemingway's Craft* (Carbondale: Southern Illinois University Press, 1973), 82-84; Barbara Korn, "Form and Idea in Hemingway's 'Big Two-Hearted River,'" *English Journal* 54 (1967): 979-81, 1014; Richard K. Peterson, *Hemingway: Direct and Oblique* (The Hague: Moutgon, 1969), 45-7; Earl H. Rovit,

Ernest Hemingway (New York: Twayne, 1963), 80-83; Julian Smith, "Hemingway and The Thing Left Out," *Journal of Modern Literature* I (1970-71): 169-82; Gregory S. Sojka, *Ernest Hemingway: The Angler as Artist* (New York: Peter Lang, 1985), 85-94; William Bysshe Stein, "Ritual in Hemingway's 'Big Two-Hearted River,'" *Texas Studies in Language and Literature* I (1960): 555-61. It should also be noted that the "traumatic" interpretations of the story had support from some statements of Hemingway about it: "If you leave out important things or events that you know about the story is strengthened . . . . 'Big Two-Hearted River' is about a boy coming home beat to the wide from a war. . . . So the war, all mention of the war, anything about the war, is omitted," "The Art of the Short Story," *Paris Review*, NO. 79 (Spring, 1981): 88. On the other hand, Wesley C. Kort, "Human Time in Hemingway's Fiction," *Modern Fiction Studies* 26 (Winter, 1980-81): 579-96, describes a general pattern in Hemingway's stories which has a hero entering a locale, confronting a situation, withdrawing from it, and reflecting as he achieves some wisdom from his encounter; Joseph M.Flora, *Hemingway's Nick Adams* (Baton Rouge: Louisiana State University Press, 1982), 145-81, gives a detailed analysis that, more than most, distances the war experience of Nick and sees a stronger strain of optimism and vitality; Tony Tanner, "Ernest Hemingway's Unhurried Sensations," *Hemingway Review* I, 2 (Spring, 1982): 20-38 (reprinted from Tanner's *Reign of Words*), stresses how Nick relishes and even prolongs every sensation nature offers as a way of achieving communion and thereby restoring himself; Keith Carabine, "'Big Two-Hearted River': A Re-interpretation," *ibid.*, 39-44, also makes Nick's euphoria the primary, but not the sole, theme of the story: his happiness is "earned because his fishing lore and his knowledge of the country are controlled by the saving grace of his determination to exact the maximum satisfaction from his pilgrimage" (42); Howard Hannum, "Soldier's Home: Immersion Therapy and Lyric Pattern in 'Big Two-Hearted River,'" *Hemingway Review* 3 (Spring, 1984): 2-13, develops an interesting integration of darker and lighter elements in an odic pattern of strophe, antistrophe, and epode. The literary success of the story, however, does not depend on the dominance of either the optimistic or pessimistic elements, but rather on the appropriate way both are developed, and that, once again, is my major concern here.

[4] See Kensi Nakajima, *"Big Two-Hearted River" as the Extreme of Hemingway's Nihilism* (Tokyo: Eichosha, 1979), who speaks of Nick's faithfulness to "models" for such acts as basic to Hemingway's ideal of expertise. However, he sees this care, as well as Nick's self-imposed deprivations, as a kind of "epicurean stoicism," the endurance of pain and delays to enhance the ensuing pleasure. He interprets this way of acting as a denial of transcendental value and so, essentially, a nihilism. This view is not unlike earlier criticism of Hemingway's anti-intellectualism: his heroes' use of sport (not to say of violence, drink, and sex) as an escape from painful memory and the futile attempt of human reason to deal with the world; see, for example, Leon Edel, "The Art of Evasion," *Folio* 20 (Spring, 1955): 18-20, and Robert Evans, "Hemingway and the Pale Cast of Thought," *American Literature* 38 (1966): 161-76. The literary question, however, is not whether Hemingway's admittedly limited code is philosophically or ethically valid, but whether it provides convincing motivation in the story, sufficient at least for a "willing suspension of disbelief" and, at best, as a consistent functioning element of the thematic structure.

[5] See Stein, 558.

[6] See Charles Fenton, *The Apprenticeship of Ernest Hemingway* (New York: Viking Press, 1954), 87-89, and Robert O.Stevens, *Hemingway's Non-Fiction* (Chapel Hill: University of North Carolina Press, 1968), 365-67, *et passim*.

[7] There are exceptions, with what seems to be a more direct connection between what is seen or done and the psychological effect—

as, for example, when Nick observes the river and finds that his disappointment over losing the big trout is draining away:

> He sat on the logs, smoking, drying in the sun, the sun warm on his back, the river shallow ahead entering the woods, curving into the woods, shallows, light glittering, big water-smooth rocks, cedars along the bank and white birches, the logs warm in the sun, smooth to sit on, without bark, gray to the touch; slowly the feeling of disappointment left him. (227)

It should be noted, too, that the irregular and embedded sequences discussed here relate to Hemingway's early attempts at an "objective correlative" in his writing, a style in which only "the sequence of motion and fact" would suggest the emotion he was trying to convey; see Ernest Hemingway, *Death in the Afternoon* (New York: Scribner's, 1932), 2, and Harry Levin, *Contexts of Criticism* (Cambridge: Harvard University Press, 1957), 155 ff. If that strict objectivity is not achieved here, at least Nick's emotions are realistically presented through their reiterated connection with the "motion and fact" of the natural setting and through the narrator's consistently close identification with Nick's perspective and, we assume, his language.

[8] On the wide use of metaphor in everyday language, see George Lakoff and Mark Johnson, *Metaphors We Live By* (Chicago: University of Chicago Press, 1980).

[9] "The succession of relatively short sentences produces a sense of rapidity or dynamism, or at times a staccato effect. This dynamism and illusion of movement is augmented by the use of almost entirely active verbs. Another technique Hemingway uses to create the effect of vitality is to play off active verbs against static ones, or employ gerundive or participial forms. The gerunds and participles are especially

important in conveying the impression of ongoing action," Grebstein, 133.

[10] On Hemingway's use in this story of his typical rhetorical links between sentences (that is, repeated words and phrases), see Waldemar Gutwinski, *Cohesion in Literary Texts* (The Hague: Mouton, 1976), 127 ff. The economy of Hemingway's transition between episodes and smaller steps of the action is worth studying; see in Part I, for example, the opening sentences of paragraphs 2, 7, 11, 16, 19, 22, and 29.

[11] Wright Morris, *The Territory Ahead* (New York: Harcourt Brace, 1958), 139.

[12] "On Writing" in *The Nick Adams Stories*, ed., Philip Young (New York: Scribner's, 1972), 239.

[13] Letter of August 15, 1924 in Carlos Baker, *Ernest Hemingway: Selected Letters* (New York: Scribner's, 1981), 122.

Flannery O'Connor: Pride and Prejudice in "The Artifical Nigger"

"The Artificial Nigger" by Flannery O'Connor reverses a traditional pattern of initiation stories and has the elder instructor achieving more wisdom than the child initiate. Mr. Head is taking his ten year old grandson to the big city to cure him of all his illusions about it and his know-it-all brashness, by revealing the evils of urban life.

The story is developed around the similarities and differences of the two main characters and their continuing efforts to get the better of one another. Despite differences of age and experience, they have a strong physical resemblance; both are also proud of their intelligence, prejudiced, talented in witty retorts. The moonlit scene which introduces them suggests the elder's view of his high moral purposes and the stand-off of their recrimination. On their train trip to the city, however, Mr. Head scores a series of major points and Nelson feels increasingly dependent on him.

> The walking tour of the city follows four increasingly
> tiring cycles during which they get lost and Mr. Head loses
> ground in the battle of wits. There are exciting experiences
> for Nelson, especially in meeting blacks, a testing which
> turns into a nasty betrayal of the boy and a crisis of
> conscience for Mr. Head, and a climactic encounter with an
> "artificial nigger" that reconciles the shame-faced guide
> and his embittered charge. The denouement returns them
> to their moonlit country home, with a new sense of human
> weakness and the need of reconciliation.
>
> The variations on the simple human relationship thus
> concluded have, however, been managed with unusual
> adroitness through levels of comedy, satire, and high seri-
> ousness and with imaginative use of elements in the setting
> (contrasts of country and city, black and white, idealizing
> moon and realistic sun) and in the thematic structure
> (Biblical and Dantean parallels, especially). And these
> disparate elements attain a satisfying unity, despite some
> extension of the narrator's remarks at the conclusion.

Flannery O'Connor's story "The Artificial Nigger" was her favorite; critics frequently refer to it as her best.[1] As an initiation narrative and a parable of salvation, it is usually compared to Hawthorne's masterpiece "My Kinsman, Major Molineux," particularly in its contrast of country and city mores, its conflict between the generations, and its moonlit scenes. But the grotesquery of "The Artificial Nigger," the tragicomedy of a Georgia rustic's painful discovery of grace, is peculiarly O'Connor's, though the subtlety of the presentation and the peaceful satisfactions of the ending are unusual in her work.

The story resembles other stories dealt with here, in suggestive ways. Like "María Concepción," it contrasts primitive psychology and values with civilized and "learned" values. Like "The Dead," it makes an effective leap from the details of a lively realism to transcendental mystery. Like "The Bear," it nominally follows the initiation of a young person to adult wisdom. But now the process is concentrated in one day, a day filled with a series of close interactions between Nelson and his grandfather. Theirs, in fact, is a recurring contention of pride and wit to see who can get the better of the other as they prepare for and go through their special trip to the city.

The relationship of the two main characters is, thus, fundamental to the story's structure. At the beginning, the stress is on their difference in the relation and the perspective is Mr. Head's (and it is *Mr.* Head throughout): his noble role is that of moral guide to his grandson; Nelson is weak and ignorant, is in need of guidance. The moon (like the narrator) is a detached and ironic observer of Mr. Head's musings, and it gives his bedroom a provocative air of dignity consonant with the old man's sense of himself. Just as the floor boards become silver and ticking becomes brocade in the miraculously transforming moonlight, Head "might have been Vergil summoned in the middle of the night to go to Dante or, better, Raphael, awakened by a blast of God's light to fly to the side of Tobias" (250).[2] By contrast, the only dark spot in the room is Nelson's pallet, where he lies asleep in the fetal position, his brand-new clothes ready at hand for his first trip—and the slop jar "made snow-white in the moonlight, appeared to stand guard over him like a small personal angel"(250).

Elements are soon introduced, however, that complicate, diminish, and, in a sense, equalize the relationship. We soon realize that the opening scene shows pride coming before the fall, that Head is smug in his moral assurance and his capability as a guide, petty in contending with his grandson, vindictive in his effort to prove that Nelson "was not as smart as he thought he was." Similarly, Nelson emerges from the innocence of sleep to demonstrate that "he was a child who was never satisfied until he had given an impudent answer" and to suggest by his scepticism and quick wit that he is a formidable judge of his grandfather's pretense to wisdom. Thus, there is good reason to shift emphasis in their development to the similarity of the main characters:

> They looked enough alike to be brothers and brothers not too far apart in age, for Mr. Head had a youthful expression by daylight while the boy's look was ancient, as if he knew everything and would be pleased to forget it. (251)

Physical characteristics reflect, of course, a deeper resemblance: grandfather and grandson share a fierce pride, a sharp wit, and common prejudices and fears about blacks and the city. In the midst of their adventure, Head accuses Nelson of "standing there grinning like a chim-pan-zee while a nigger woman gives you directions" (263). But in the full glare of the sun in which "everything looked exactly what it was," it is Head who is "hunched like an old monkey on the garbage can lid" (264). And in the moment of crisis, it is "his own image and likeness" that Head denies. With the break in their relationship, there is a modulation back to difference and separateness, and it is only with reconciliation that their fundamental identity is reasserted: "Mr. Head looked like an ancient child and Nelson like a miniature old man" (269).

The brief excursion of Mr. Head and Nelson to the city provides an ample frame for their series of contentions and for the alternating and overlapping series of encounters with others that progressively redefine their relationship. The story's exposition and first stage is presented in the bedroom scene and later at the breakfast table. As the setting is sketched out, emphasis is on the isolation of the principals, the simplicity, familiarity, and relative sufficiency of their surroundings, and these features contrast with some of the hardships to be encountered in the city. The matters the characters argue about are seriocomic and petty instances of what later became broader themes of dependence and autonomy, knowledge and ignorance: whether Nelson had indeed been to the city before (presumably Atlanta) or has reason to take pride in it as his birthplace; whether Head had been to the city often enough to be a safe guide; whether Nelson will recognize a black person when he sees one for the first time. On every point, Nelson has a sceptical and sometimes a witty answer. To Head's challenge "Have you ever seen me lost?", for example, his pointed reply is "It's nowhere around here to get lost at." And the prepositional complication is at once a convincing bit of dialogue and a comic suggestion of the involuted process by which they do get lost.

While it presents their anticipations, the first section of the story also establishes the basic anxieties of the characters—about the city itself and its possible evils and dangers, about getting lost, about the city's Negroes most especially. It also introduces a strain of implication (to be orchestrated more fully later, especially with Dantean parallels) by dignifying Head's mission with literary and Biblical allusion and by erecting over the whole scene the machinery of the moon as observer-participant. It is in these elements that the narrator's somewhat distant and initially satiric point of view is set.

The train trip to the city constitutes the second stage of the narrative. It serves principally to build anticipation, to specify further some of Nelson's anxieties, and to prepare Mr. Head for his eventual fall. As he is confronted with alien situations, Nelson begins to doubt himself and, temporarily at least, to fall into greater dependency on his grandfather. When he fails to recognize his "first nigger" on the train, he wonders for the first time whether he "might be inadequate to the day's expectations" (256). After Head foils the haughty waiter with his remark about cockroaches, Nelson feels

> a sudden keen pride in him. He realized the old man would be his only support in the strange place they were approaching. He would be entirely alone in the world if he were ever lost from his grandfather. A terrible excitement shook him and he wanted to take hold of Mr. Head's coat and hold on like a child. (257)

Again, when he is pulled back to his seat at the suburban station, he understood for the first time in his life "that his grandfather was indispensable to him" (257). And as Nelson's dependence increases, Head's temporary triumphs prepare ironically for his series of errors in the city.

A central element in his fall, as we shall see, is his surprised discovery of his true person, his recognition of possibilities within himself that he had not realized. That aspect of the major epiphany is prepared from the beginning in the ambivalent characterization of Head under the gaze of the moon. But during the train trip, uncertainty about identity is significantly increased, especially in contrasts between reality and appearances, frequently ghostly appearances, and in distorted reflections. As Head and Nelson approach their train stop in the morning, their highly personalized moon has become "a grey transparent moon, hardly stronger than a thumb-print"; trains passing that spot *appeared* "to emerge from a tunnel of trees, and, hit for a second by the cold sky, vanish terrified into the woods again"; as they wait for the train, they "stared ahead as if they were awaiting an apparition" (252). When they are seated, they see their own "ghost-like" faces in the window.

At the same time, their personal identities tend to be ignored by others on the train, whose reaction is, at most, indifferent. The conductor "did not look as if it mattered one way or the other if they got on or not" (253). The traveler across the aisle goes to sleep when Head tries to engage him in conversation. The waiter who asks them to stand aside does so "with an airy wave of the arm as if he were brushing aside flies" (256). This indifference does not deter Head, however; he is noisy, brash, unwavering in his didactic mission which, nominally a caring for Nelson, more basically advertises his superior knowledge again. He tells Nelson where to sit ("Nobody cares if you sit there"), instructs him in the importance of tickets, the mysteries of plumbing on the train, and the location of stations. In more crucial matters, his catechizing, after the passage of Nelson's "first nigger" in such splendor, leaves its bitter residue of prejudice and his witty retort to the black waiter, of false security. But the straight and narrow path to which Head had brought his grandson, the railroad track which brings the pair with such ominous smoothness and efficiency to the city, multiplies and criss-crosses at the terminal in a confusion which fitly introduces them to the day's adventure.

Since some of the basic natural patterns of the story are circular (a journey from home and back, from the early morning moon to the evening moon), there is some appropriateness in having the tourists' exploration of the city start in roughly circular paths. There are four sweeps that constitute this central section of the narrative: to the black shoeshine stand, to the black woman who gives Nelson directions, to the white woman felled by Nelson, to the white man who gives Head directions. Each portion of the journey provides opportunities for instruction about places or persons encountered (stores, fortune-telling scales, sewers, black people, streetcar tracks) or for unexpected enlightenment. Each yields matter, too, for continuing recrimination. But on the train and in the first circling of the city, there are increments to Mr. Head's pride in his experience and knowledge (though his knowledge is sometimes the fruit of earlier humiliating experience) and corresponding increases in Nelson's sense of dependence. But in the second circling and the discovery that they are indeed lost and have lost their lunch bag too, Nelson temporarily has the advantage.

At the same time, the rather narrow range of emotive meanings, most related to shame and anxiety, is broadened and deepened as the climaxes of the story are prepared. Aside from his recurrent irritation with his grandfather and his brief delight in seeing the city's stores, Nelson's deepest emotional moments are in his reactions to blacks. His first sight of one and his humbling by his grandfather on the occasion had left him with a "fierce raw fresh hate," and now, passing the houses of blacks, and under their constant gaze, his "skin began to prickle." But when he finally brings himself to ask directions from the large colored woman standing in her doorway, his reaction is quite different. Without experience or memory of his own mother, he is drawn intensely by the overwhelming physical and sexual presence of this earth mother:

> He stood drinking in every detail of her. His eyes traveled up from her great knees to her forehead and then made a triangular path from the glistening sweat on her neck down and across her tremendous bosom and over her bare arm to where her fingers lay hidden

in her hair. He suddenly wanted her to reach down
and pick him up and draw him against her and then
he wanted to feel her breath on his face. He wanted to
look down and down into her eyes while she held him
tighter and tighter. He had never had such a feeling
before. He felt as is he were reeling down through a
pitch-black tunnel. (262)

While this experience with the black woman clearly represents a reversal of earlier feelings,[3] it does not appear to be sustained for Nelson in any radical change of his racial prejudice. While the possibility is not ruled out, especially in the third climactic experience with "the artificial nigger," neither is it spelled out, in the fashion that Head's conversion from pride is, for example. But given Nelson's age, especially, it might not have been inappropriate to leave the question open and pending. And this seems to be the import of references to his later sleep troubled by "black forms moving up from some dark part of him into the light" (264) and, at a more critical juncture, to his rather weak impulse to forgive his grandfather: "he felt, from some remote place inside himself, a black mysterious form reach up as if it would melt his frozen vision in one hot grasp" (267).

The major turning point of the story is also a moment of troubled emotion, of fear in Nelson and then cold contempt, of unexpected fear in Head and then bitter shame. His grandfather's tricky attempt to bring Nelson to a sense of complete ignorance and loss recoils on himself and brings him to that impasse instead. As he comes upon the scene of Nelson's accident with the woman, he senses constriction, impending imprisonment: the crowd surrounds and threatens him; a policeman has been called for and is, perhaps, approaching; Nelson clings to him tightly. When, in his cowardice, he says he does not know Nelson, however, he feels isolated—the circle of women draws back, Nelson relinquishes his hold, and he walks on alone. He feels the enormity of his denial immediately as he hangs his head in shame, and he feels it confirmed by Nelson's unforgiving stare, "two small eyes piercing into his back like pitchfork prongs."

Head's reaction and the infernal imagery which develops it may seem comically exaggerated.[4] But his treason will be seen to be an exemplar of the general sinfulness that radically needs God's mercy, and his fall is rendered precisely and appropriately in the Dantesque pattern of the story's symbols. For Dante does put those who betray their kinsmen in the very lowest circle of hell, sunk in ice, with heads bowed before the icy gale. And his appeasing offers of Coca-Cola or spigot water to his grandson are unavailing, for Nelson's "mind had frozen around his grandfather's treachery as if he were trying to preserve it intact to present it at the final judgment" (267). Having lost sight of the station dome and now of the car tracks in a suburb with big white houses "like partially submerged icebergs" and driveways that "wound around and around in endless ridiculous circles," Head is clearly in a hell of his own making. Wandering in "a black strange place where nothing was like it had ever been before," Head "felt that if he saw a sewer entrance he would drop into it and let himself be carried away" (267).

But as usual in O'Connor's stories of salvation in unexpected, not to say violent, circumstances, "the guilty, suffering spirit is a more likely recipient of grace than the apathetic soul smugly entrenched in notions of its own moral superiority."[5] Before that moment of grace, however, and the major climax of the story, there is a buildup which is as emotionally rich, difficult, and reversionary as Head's progress to this point. There is first his humbling admission that he is lost ("Oh Gawd, I'm lost!"), the glimmer of hope after he gets directions ("We're going to get home!") which is dashed by Nelson's "triumphantly cold" stare, and finally the unforeseen moment of relief and reconciliation before the "artificial nigger." The battered plaster statue of a Negro, who looked too miserable to tell whether he was, like the Heads, "meant to be old or young," is not a symbol of pride nor of Satan. It is rather a grotesque image of the "agony" from which mercy grows. It is a reminder of the misery of blacks under the pride and prejudice of white dominance, and, with appropriate irony ("We didn't come to look at niggers," Mr. Head had said earlier), it brings grandfather and grandson together in acknowledging their fall and redeems them from their pride and, perhaps less clearly, even from their prejudice.[6] The reconciliation of Mr. Head and Nelson is developed principally in a return to the imagery of their similarities:

"An artificial nigger!" Nelson repeated in Mr. Head's exact tone.

The two of them stood there with their necks forward at almost the same angle and their shoulders curved in almost exactly the same way and their hands trembling identically in their pockets. Mr. Head looked like an ancient child and Nelson like a miniature old man. They stood gazing at the artificial Negro as if they were faced with some great mystery, some monument to another's victory that brought them together in their common defeat. They could both feel it dissolving their differences like an action of mercy. (268-69)

"The thing to do with a boy," Head said earlier to the man on the train, "is to show him all it is to show. Don't hold nothing back" (254). At this climax of "showing," Nelson's hopeful look is at once a declaration of new dependence (to an elder with his own sense of dependence on God just aborning) and also an appeal to explain the statue and, thereby, "to explain once and for all the mystery of existence." Head's answer, in its witty irony, may be appropriate to that suburban neighborhood. If, however, it is woefully inadequate to the question of racism, or suffering, or the grand mystery of life, that is something that Head seems to be aware of and that Nelson, in the measured way of his forgiveness, chooses to overlook:

> Mr. Head opened his lips to make a lofty statement and heard himself say, "They ain't got enough real ones here. They got to have an artificial one."
>
> After a second, the boy nodded, with a strange shivering about his mouth, and said, "Let's go home before we get ourselves lost again". (269)

The final action of grace comes in a denouement with their return to the relative innocence of the country.[7] Accumulated images of constriction and direction (tunnels, tubes, sewers, streets, tracks) give way to freer images of spaciousness and free motion ("the moon . . . sprang from a cloud and flooded the clearing with light," "the sky . . . was hung with gigantic white clouds illuminated like lanterns"). The circle of the journey is completed with repeated details of the moon "restored to its full splendor" or the train disappearing "like a frightened serpent into the woods." What the moonlight creates now, however, as Preston Browning remarks, is a real garden with protecting walls, not a castle of illusion and pride.[8] In that light, the narrator emerges as the real guide of the story, the angel of a god who "afflicts and shows mercy," who "leads down to Hades and brings up again" (Tobias 13:2), the Vergil who has brought his hero through the Inferno and Purgatorio to the gates of the Paradiso.

Some critics have objected to the extent of the "editorializing" on Head's conversion (and one might wish that it were more brief), to the use of theological categories beyond his knowledge or experience, to the change of tone.[9] There are indeed some changes in the closing paragraphs of the story, but they are not completely untoward or unprepared. The commentary here, for example, is about the same length as the analysis of Nelson's experience before the black woman or of Head's sense of loss after his betrayal. That the statements now are more abstract, general—and theological—is clear enough. But pressures for meaningful explanation have been built gradually and forcefully through the story. What *is* new now is the emergence into fuller view of the narrator as analytic observer. In the beginning of the story, this personality is more tentative and playful, as, for example, in the picture of the moon as participant or the extension of pathetic fallacy even to the servant-chair ("which *might* have been brocade," "*as if* it were waiting for his permission," "Mr. Head *could* have said"—emphasis added) or in the ambivalent portrait of Head himself. There is detachment here, the edge of keen mockery. Even when the tone becomes, in the main stretch of the narrative, more business-like and neutral, the satire continues in careful modulations which do much to unify the story. It is an essential part of the continuing reversals, of the play of rustic grotesquery against Dantesque sublimity, of pettifogging and aimless wandering against human and transcendental mystery, and all of this makes the traditional salvation journey distinctively comic and serious. But as John Cunningham has observed, O'Connor's satire is "an agent of compassion" and her irony, "the means of discovering the complex nature of good and evil in her characters."[10] Thus, if new definiteness and explicitness mark the narrator's final comments, so, too, does a sympathetic identification with the hero in the universal experience of a troubled soul feeling the relief of forgiveness. Nelson, the "other" observer of Mr. Head at this point, is brought to such sympathy, too: "even his face lightened" and he muttered his own conclusion to his experience. But, in a final and kindly reversal, he also speaks to his grandfather's needs as he sees them, and drops his claim that he had been to the city before: "I'm glad I've went once, but I'll never go back again!"

Thus, in the seesawing antagonism of the two main characters, betrayal, the consciousness of sin, and the agony of guilt have brought Mr. Head to overcome his pride—and Nelson, to a similar achievement. Whether their prejudice against blacks has been as successfully transcended is left in some doubt, for what the "artificial nigger" has more clearly absolved is their prejudice for one another. Nevertheless, in their newfound understanding and sympathy, the complex dance of their similarities and differences in the story is brought to a satisfying close.

Notes

[1] For general commentary on the story, see especially Preston M. Browning, Jr., *Flannery O'Connor* (Carbondale: Southern Illinois University Press, 1974), 60-69; David Eggenschwiler, *The Christian Humanism of Flannery O'Connor* (Detroit: Wayne State University Press, 1972), 85-91; Kathleen Feeley, *Flannery O'Connor: Voice of the Peacock* (New Brunswick: Rutgers University Press, 1972), 120-24; Lorine Getz, *Nature and Grace in Flannery O'Connor's Fiction* (New York: Edwin Mellen Press, 1982), 47-58; Carter Martin, *The True Country: Themes in the Fiction of Flannery O'Connor* (Nashville: Vanderbilt University Press, 1969), 112-16, 148-51; Gilbert Muller, *Nightmares and Visions*

Flannery O'Connor 159

(Athens: University of Georgia Press, 1972), 71-75; Carol Schloss, *Flannery O'Connor's Dark Comedies* (Baton Rouge: Louisiana State University Press, 1980), 118-23; and Dorothy Walters, *Flannery O'Connor* (New York: Twayne Publishers, 1973), 106-07, 118-21.

[2] Numbers in parentheses refer to pages of "The Artificial Nigger" in *Flannery O'Connor: The Complete Stories* (New York: Farrar,Straus & Giroux, 1979).

[3] The story is characterized by numerous reversals, of course. They occur in small details like Mr. Head's theory that Nelson's weight is incorrect on his ticket because the machine had printed the number upside down or, in much more significant matters, as when the same scale opines that Head is "upright and brave." In the development of the central irony, we are alerted early in the story by the failure of Head's determination to be up before Nelson, and we are reminded frequently by his repeated assertions that he knows the city and won't get lost. The ending spells out in detail how it is Head rather than Nelson who has been morally instructed by their visit.

[4] On the pattern of Dantean and Biblical allusions, see Peter Hayes "Dante, Tobit, and 'The Artificial Nigger,'" *Studies in Short Fiction* 5 (1968): 263-68, and Gilbert Muller, "The City of Woe: Flannery O'Connor's Dantean Vision," *Georgia Review* 23 (1969): 206-13, though the latter multiplies possible parallels excessively.

[5] Dorothy Walters, 37.

[6] "In the face of this final mystery, both Nelson and Mr. Head are confounded and made equal by 'this monument to another's victory,' and, as equalizer, the statue becomes a medium of grace. The marvelous appropriateness of this—that the Negro, a traditional symbol in the American South of inequality among men, should be the agent effecting an acknowledgement of essential human equality—can scarcely be exaggerated and that it should be a chipped plaster figure, with 'a wild

look of misery,' which serves as the agent of human reconciliation and as a sign of the magnitude of God's mercy, is appropriate also. For this 'crucified' Negro, made of clay and grotesque in the contrast of its intended expression of happiness and its actual look of affliction, constitutes an analogue of the Christian belief that the lowly, the despised, the insignificant ('the least of these') may well be the chosen means of divine revelation" (Browning, 68-69). See also Brainard Cheney, "Miss O'Connor Creates Unusual Humor Out of Ordinary Sin," *Sewanee Review* 71 (1963): 651; Richard Coleman, "Flannery O'Connor: A Scrutiny of Two Forms of Her Many-Leveled Art," *Phoenix* (1966): 55; and especially George Cheatham, "Jesus, O'Connor's Artificial Nigger," *Studies in Short Fiction* 22 (1985): 475-79, who argues specifically that "the statue, crucified as it is on the wall, symbolizes Jesus Christ."

[7] See James Goss, "The Double Action of Mercy in 'The Artificial Nigger,'" *Christianity and Literature* 23, iii (1975): 36-45.

[8] Browning, 65-66; see also William Rodney Allen, "Mr. Head and Hawthorne: Allusion and Conversion in Flannery O'Connor's 'The Artificial Nigger,'" *Studies in Short Fiction* 21 (1984): 17-23, who discusses the opening of O'Connor's story in relation to a moonlit scene in Hawthorne's "The Custom House," but neglects the more basic influence of "My Kinsman, Major Molineux."

[9] See, for example, Thomas Lorch, "Flannery O'Connor: A Christian Allegorist," *Critique* 10 (1968): 76-77; and Miles Orvell, *Invisible Parade: the Fiction of Flannery O'Connor* (Philadelphia: Temple University Press, 1972), 158-59; A.R. Coulthard, "From Sermon to Parable: Four Conversion Stories by Flannery O'Connor," *American Literature* 55 (1983): 58-63. O'Connor herself felt that, in some sense, she may have gone too far ("from the Garden of Eden to the Gates of Paradise") in the conclusion; see her letter to Ben Griffith in *The Habit of Being*, ed. Sally Fitzgerald (New York: Farrar, Straus & Giroux, 1979), 78. But

the closing paragraphs have been defended in various ways. See, for example, Louis D. Rubin, Jr., "Flannery O'Connor's Company of Southeners Or, 'The Artificial Nigger' Read as Fiction Rather Than Theology," *A Gallery of Southeners* (Baton Rouge: Louisiana State University Press, 1982), 129-34, who sees the passage as "not only appropriate but necessary, for not merely the final episode but *the entire story* has been told that way, from outside and above, by a narrator whose descriptive commentary not only goes far beyond Mr. Head's verbal and conceptual limitations but works with and against the actual mundane situation throughout, for purposes of comedy and pathos." On the other hand, W.F. Monroe, "Flannery O'Connor's Sacramental Icon: 'The Artificial Nigger,'" *South Central Review* 1 (Winter, 1984): 74-77, thinks that Mr. Head is portrayed as sure now of being saved as he was earlier, of being wise—and so is now risking another fall.

[10] John Cunningham, "Recent Works on Flannery O'Connor," *Southern Humanities Review* 8 (1974): 386.

Eudora Welty: "Powerhouse" and The Mystery of Art

Eudora Welty's "Powerhouse" describes the reactions of several audiences to the exuberant artistry of a black jazz musician who resembles the great Fats Waller. What is common to these reactions is a curiosity about the sources of Powerhouse's craft, as both a musician and a storyteller.

The narrative is divided into six parts, the smaller parts flanking the two central sections. The first two introduce Powerhouse as pianist and band leader, detailing his style in the dance concert for a white Mississippi audience. The enthusiastic narrator concludes them with an invitation to study the secret of his magic, especially his improvisational skills. The third section introduces a new talent, as Powerhouse entertains his side men with some sketchy suggestions of a tragicomedy involving his wife and one Uranus Knockwood. In the fourth and largest part, Powerhouse embroiders this story during a break at the local tavern and, with his band members collaborating, entertains the poor

> blacks who have followed him from the dance hall with amusing and "scary" variations of his theme.
>
> The two final sections are denouement. Powerhouse and the band conclude the story of the shadowy villain and the suicidal wife, as they return to the dance hall followed by a crowd "afraid they will die laughing." And Powerhouse, after an elaborate set of variations on "Somebody Loves Me," hints at what the real secret of his art is.
>
> While there is some echo of the music in the improvisational brilliance of the storytelling, the more general concern of the story is with the mystery of art itself and the response which it requires. It is with a skill comparable to her hero's that Welty develops a balance between Powerhouse's different skills and contrasts the reactions of his audience.

Eudora Welty's "Powerhouse" is a lyric celebration of a jazz pianist and band leader modeled after the great Fats Waller. The story celebrates the intoxicating power of the musician's performance, of his intricate and seemingly inexhaustible improvisation, of his larger-than-life appearance and dramatic presence. But the story is more basically concerned with mystery—the mystery of art itself and, to a lesser degree, the mystery of race. The animated descriptions of the story, then, move between the personality of Powerhouse and his music and the reactions of his various audiences—in the dance hall, the band itself, the World Café. And these descriptions swing between ambiguity and ambivalence: on the one hand, the ambiguous relations of joy and sorrow, of fantasy and realism in the black personality, and of primitivism and sophistication, originality and convention in his music; on the other hand, the ambivalence of enjoyment and curiosity and, on the part of the whites, of acceptance and fear. Thus, the basic elements repeated in the story are descriptions of the mysterious Powerhouse and his virtuoso performances and of various reactions to him. "Powerhouse is playing! He's on tour from the city . . . " is the sequence of exclamation and description that begins the story, and in various extensions and combinations of these two elements, description and reaction, the story proceeds. Furthermore, as most of the story's analysts have recognized, Welty attempts to echo features of the music itself, especially as she develops an elaborate parallel between the improvisational brilliance of the jazz and of Powerhouse's own storytelling.

Welty has divided the narrative into six parts, setting them off with additional spacing and balancing the smaller sections around the two larger, central parts. The first two sections (131-32, 132-33) are a general introduction, one sketching the appearance of Powerhouse, the second, his style and method in presenting the dance concert this rainy evening in Alligator, Mississippi.[1]

Almost immediately we are told that there "is no one in the world like him." And so the difficulty of describing the absolutely unique is made to account for the rush of exaggerated and ambiguous detail, of widely varied similes and metaphors which follow in the excited attempt to evoke the presence of the man. Initially the emphasis is on the enormous size of Powerhouse—a "virtual Negro Paul Bunyan," says Alfred Appel[2]—but then on his primitive and exotic racial characteristics, on the constant movement in his performance that seems obscene, on the seemingly independent life of his accomplished fingers. The imagery is dominantly visual: the rich array of comparisons involves animal (lizard, monkey) but also domestic (platter, kneading dough) elements, and as Powerhouse becomes entranced in his own music, an important strain of water images begins.[3] In the course of the story, Powerhouse is presented as an energy source for band and audience; a monkey; a devil; an Asiatic, Jewish, Babylonian, Peruvian, coffee-colored giant, with "African feet of the greatest size"; a teacher quieting down a classroom; a machine with "piston legs" in constant motion; a tropical tree with banana fingers; a captain washed overboard into a whirlpool of his own music, hailing the members of his band; a musician-mystic, listening to his own variations with "a look of hideous, powerful rapture on his face"; a fanatic; a pianist laying "his finger on a key with the promise and serenity of a sibyl touching the book." The contradictions and ambiguities of the description (while they are dominated by a joyful response related precisely to the fact that, above all, Powerhouse is "a person of joy") raise questions about perspective. Perhaps the best that be said is that the narrator combines the varied perceptions of a very sensitive observer (clearly as high on the music and its leader as the band is) with the more ambivalent and even prejudiced reactions of the general audience, the latter to be more clearly differentiated as the story proceeds.

As the first section ends, therefore, the distinction between sensitive and insensitive listener is drawn more explicitly, as a basic reason is advanced for recounting the events of this evening's dance-concert. For the narrator is not simply high on the music, she is curious about the mysterious sources of its power. So she asks other sensitive listeners to join her in observing and studying the performance—"to learn what it is."

The challenge, it seems, is to analyze not simply the band's music but also "the least word, especially what they say to one another"(132). The hypothesis, then, is that the key to the band's achievement will somehow be discovered in their verbal exchanges. But actually what the narrator wants to observe is what the musicians say to each other "in another language." The last phrase could be construed more broadly: the other language could be the artistic process itself, speaking to others in that language could be interacting with them in the process—as in a band or an acrobatic team. Both the usual and adapted sense of "words" and "saying" do, in fact, seem to be used in the beautifully accurate accounts of how Powerhouse produces his verbal and musical hallucinations and of how he ultimately confounds the curiosity of the simple and the hypotheses of more sophisticated observers. What we will have, again, are detailed descriptions of the magical processes and briefer reports of how Powerhouse's audiences respond and probe for explanations.

But, again, it is not simply Powerhouse's music which will figure in this alternation. Miss Welty, wisely enough as it turns out, does not limit herself to the music itself or explicit consideration of the improvisation. Rather the emphasis is on the dramatics of the performance. The chief performer is the constant focus—not his own playing necessarily, but more his apparently artless direction of the band, his benevolent encouragement of his principals (and of the audience), his total absorption as he guides the group through its incredible improvisations.[4] And later these same emphases will characterize Powerhouse's storytelling.

In the second section of the narrative, the emphasis is on Powerhouse as leader: receiving written requests; indicating his selections to the band; getting them set ("You-all ready to do some serious walking?"); directing them with a brief signal or a shout; inviting the sidemen out and encouraging them; maneuvering the whole band through endless choruses—and pouring it all out "in the greatest delight and brutality." But he is not, it is repeated, a show-off. He loves the music, the way the band plays, even, it seems, the audience, as he looks down "so benevolently" on all their faces and whispers the lyrics to them.

After this elaborate description of the performance, there are only brief notes on the audience reaction: a few dance, most crowd around Powerhouse and watch spellbound, but there is ambivalence:

> Sometimes they steal glances at one another, as if to say, Of course, you know how it is with *them*—Negroes—band leaders—they would play the same way, giving all they've got, for an audience of one. . . . When somebody, no matter who, gives everything, it makes people feel ashamed for him. (133)

Despite the step-by-step account of this section, the careful tracing of such wild and happy movement, the sources of Powerhouse's art remain a secret. The closed eye and masked face are as much a symbol of that hermetic mystery as of black defensiveness before a white audience ("Powerhouse reads each one, studying with a secret face. . . . Then a light shines under his eyelids. . . . Valentine, who plays with his eyes shut"). But the exalted joy of the jazz can open eyes as well as mouths ("O Lord, say the distended eyes from beyond the boundary of the trumpets, Hello and good-bye . . . such a leer for everybody. . . . Powerhouse looks out kindly from behind the piano; he opens his mouth. . . . He'll smile and say 'Beautiful'" [132-133]).

The third section introduces a new dimension of Powerhouse's art. Against the background of "the one waltz they will even consent to play—by request, 'Pagan Love Song,'" and presumably with less to keep track of, Powerhouse entertains his sidemen with some patter. He offers them the kernel of a surprising and tragic story: he's got a telegram announcing that his wife is dead. And the telegram has been signed by a shadowy figure, Uranus Knockwood.

It is quickly apparent, however, that the report is fiction, not fact—though the question of its truth will be returned to frequently. Commentators have suggested that the story may at least imply Powerhouse's own loneliness, or his fear that in her loneliness, his wife Gypsy may be unfaithful, or that he may eventually lose her, or that he feels alienated and exploited simply as a black or more especially as a black artist whose jazz style is stolen and capitalized on by other, presumably white, musicians like Knockwood, that "nogood, pussyfooted crooning creeper, that follow around after me, coming up like weeds behind me, following around after me . . . on the trail I leave . . . sings my songs, gets close to my agent like a Betsy-bug . . . "(137-8).[5]

However, while Powerhouse's report does enlarge the story's subdued counterpoint of the tragic, what is emphasized at this point is rather its playful treatment by the band. As the leader feeds his principals bits of the theme, they respond sceptically—and their alternating give-and-take creates a new series of variations paralleling the improvisations of their music:

> "Uranus Knockwood is the name signed." Powerhouse lifts his eyes open. "Ever heard of him?" A bubble shoots out on his lip like a plate on a counter.
>
> Valentine is beating slowly on with his palm and scratching the strings with his long blue nails. He is fond of a waltz. Powerhouse interrupts him.
>
> "I don't know him. Don't know who he is." Valentine shakes his head with the closed eyes.

"Say it again."

"Uranus Knockwood."

"That ain't Lenox Avenue."

"It ain't Broadway."

"Ain't ever seen it wrote out in any print, even for horse racing."

"Hell, that's on a star, boy, ain't it?" Crash of the cymbals. (134)

Worked into such series there are echoes that sustain the notion that a close parallelism is being developed between story and jazz, and they continue in the next section: the opening questions ("You-all ready? . . . You know what happened to me?"); the compositional pattern of words and music ("Tell me, tell me, tell me.' He makes triplets, and begins a new chorus."); the repeated chorus itself ("You say you got a telegram.' This is Valentine, patient and sleepy, beginning again."); the increasing detail of variations (Powerhouse is elaborate. 'Yas, the time I go out, go way downstairs a long cor-ri-dor to . . .").

But more fundamental to the evolving parallel of blues tale and jazz are the rapid tempo and exclamatory excitement of Eudora Welty's writing. Thus, the opening section spills out in a series of short clauses, typically punctuated with dashes—the kind of hurried shorthand used by a reporter trying to capture the living scene ("don't let them escape you"). And the series plays its exotic variety of descriptions against a steady beat of references to the hero ("he . . . him . . . he . . . his . . . He's . . .

"[131]) and—with a climactic flurry of questions and commands—to the addressee summoned to see him as he is.

This ebullience is carried into the third section. However, the generalized statements that frame the section and the orderly sequence in which Powerhouse's method is presented slow the pace, though they allow for the build-up of emphasis within separate stages of the concert being described. There is a further slowdown as the music dawdles over a waltz in the third section, but the rhythm of assertion and objection in the Gypsy story gives promise of new excitement, even as it creates new uncertainties.[6]

The variations on Gypsy's suicide are expanded and brought to a magical climax in the fourth and longest section of the story (135-139). After a run through the drenching rain, Powerhouse and his sidemen enter the World Cafe for some beer, some banter with the waitress, and then some entertainment for the admiring crowd of a "hundred dark, ragged, silent, delighted Negroes" who were listening outside the dance hall and have now followed them. Powerhouse's role as magician now becomes more explicit as he draws one or another item from his capacious pocket: a large towel (at the end of the third part, that is), mints for Little Brother, a "million nickels" for the nickelodeon (making the last one disappear). Later he will threaten to take from the same hiding place the infamous Knockwood telegram to prove the "truth" of his story.

But his more essential magic is what delights the waitress and the crowd, his "talk and scares." Again, there are indications that the blues tale and its variations are meant to parallel the jazz: Powerhouse's call for quiet ("Listen!"), the extended hands as he begins, the whispering, the final call to "get out of here," the intermission is up. If there are to be good "scares," there has to be a messy death: Gypsy has to jump and "bust her brains all over the world"—and the scene has to be conjured up convincingly. If there is to be good "talk," there has to be surprise, variation, exaggeration, humor—all elements, that is, of good jazz improvisation. And Powerhouse is able and willing to supply all these elements, ably assisted by his principals.[7] As the Gypsy story is now developed in four choruses, it takes on hints of loneliness, despair, betrayal, adultery, which may, again, be projections of Powerhouse's real concerns but are certainly the basic material of traditional blues. What clearly dominates here, in any case, is the humor of the performance, as in the hilarious responsory about the villain Knockwood:

"You know him."

"Uranus Knockwood!"

"Yeahhh!"

"He take our wives when we gone!"

"He come in when we goes out!"

"Uh-huh!"

"He go out when we comes in!"

"Yeahhh!"

"He standing behind the door!"

"Old Uranus Knockwood."

"You know him."

Eudora Welty 173

"Middle-sized man."

"Wears a hat."

"That's him." (138)

Again, after an elaborate description of a performance, there is a brief reference to the reaction of the audience, clearly the most responsive audience of the evening: "Everybody in the room moans with pleasure."

Before the performance draws to a close, there are two seemingly unrelated incidents. A local folk hero is introduced to the musicians, a "great loggy Negro with bursting eyes" who has pulled up fourteen white people drowned in a boat accident on July Creek; and the waitress has an exchange with Powerhouse about the "truth" of his story. An uncomfortable silence follows the introduction of the hero, and it can be attributed to the half-brother who has brought him forward as a contribution to the proceedings but, in contrast to Powerhouse, has undercut the effect of his story by straightforward explanation: "Can't even swim. Done it by holding his breath." Not too different, then, is the waitress's simple effort to explain the effect of Powerhouse's story: "It must be the real truth." But the jazz man will not be trapped into betraying the mystery of his art; he sidesteps the question and suggests another variation with an even better "scare":

> "No, babe, it ain't the truth." His eyebrows fly up, and he begins to whisper to her out of his vast oven mouth. His hand stays in his pocket. "Truth is something worse, I ain't said what, yet. It's something hasn't come to me, but I ain't saying it won't. And when it does, then want me to tell you?" He sniffs all at once,

his eyes come open and turn up, almost too far. He is dreamily smiling.

"Don't, boss, don't, Powerhouse!"

"Oh!" the waitress screams.

"Go on git out of here!" bellows Powerhouse, taking his hand out of his pocket and clapping after her red dress.

The ring of watchers breaks and falls away. (139)

The two final sections of the story are denouement. Returning to the dance hall, Powerhouse concludes the Gypsy story with a telegram concocted for Knockwood, something that will reach him "and come out the other side." For Powerhouse still has a conjurer's control over him ("I got him now! I got my eye on him," he had indicated in the seance over the ketchup bottle). The crowd following "are afraid they will die laughing" at Powerhouse's final embellishment, as well as at the band's last set of variations as they spell Uranus Knockwood's name "all the ways it could be spelled." And the theme of Powerhouse's volcanic energy returns. As he throws back his head in the rain, a "look of hopeful desire seems to blow somehow like vapor from his dilated nostrils over his face"; he rejects the anticlimactic literalism of Scoot—to call Gypsy, raises his arm in the rain, and receives the exaggerated praise of Little Brother about his voice.

Back in the dance hall, there is more dancing among the white audience, but ambivalence continues: the jitterbugs may respond to the superb jazz but the elderly couples go their own way "undisturbed and stately." The extraordinary skills of Powerhouse are, nevertheless, emphasized again. He tunes up with the band with "falsetto growls," gets his piano back under control with "outrageous force," smiles again at "something glimmering and fragile." As the picture of great musician is re-established, the narrator returns to her initial thesis. What has rehearsing the words of Powerhouse and the band or the cafe crowd revealed? What has been shown in tracing the interactions of his musical or verbal magic? Well, says the narrator finally, "who could ever remember any of the things he says." They are just inspired remarks that roll out of his mouth like smoke" (141). We could object that the narrator herself has done a remarkably good job of remembering, but we would probably agree with her implied conclusion that the original hypothesis should be dropped; neither directly nor indirectly will the mystery of art be revealed by the words of the artist nor can it be fully deduced from the interactions of the performance itself.

There is finally, however, the extended presentation of "Somebody Loves Me." Powerhouse has "already done twelve or fourteen choruses, piling them up nobody knows how." With the ultimate puzzle—"Somebody loves me, I wonder who!"—there comes, in a wonderfully balanced but syncopated series of lyric word and gesture (a b, a b b, b a), the glimmer of an answer:

> "Maybe . . . " He uses all his right hand on a trill.
> "Maybe . . . " He pulls back his spread fingers, and looks out upon the place where he is. A vast, impersonal and yet furious grimace transfigures his wet face.
>
> ". . . Maybe it's you!" (141)

This answer is not for the white audience of the dance hall in general. Its response to the volcanic talent of Powerhouse has been too restrained and ambivalent, nothing like that of the band's principals, the waitress screaming "delicately with pleasure," the poor blacks stirring with halloos of laughter and sighs of happiness—and all contributing their small share to the creative process.[8] Rather, the typical thought of the white audience has been that when "*somebody, no matter who*, gives everything, it makes *people* feel ashamed for him." (133; emphasis added). But maybe there is that isolated individual (like the narrator), maybe a few (like the addressees of the story), maybe, in fact, "you," who take Powerhouse himself, his abundantly joyful and sometimes suffering art, his universal benevolence—who take all these realities for what they are and give no less in return.

"Love" as the key to the paradoxes of Powerhouse—his mythic and human face, his brute force and tenderness, to the mysteries of his complicated arts and of art itself, to his own racial experience and of racial tension in general—may seem oversimplified and hackneyed. That the idea fits the ending with such ease and sureness indicates that it is a reality seen clearly and deeply in itself and, more importantly, in its relevance to the problems and expectations raised here. "Love," says Elizabeth Evans, "is the most characteristic word of Eudora Welty's writing, but it is a word shorn of sentimentality."[9] She brings us to the word here only through clearly demonstrated facts about Powerhouse—that he surrenders himself to his music because he loves it and that he gives everything he's got to an audience because he also loves people.[10]

That love ends the story is the result of both happy accident and of deftly controlled writing. The accident is that "Somebody Loves Me" was substituted after the original material from "Hold Tight" ("fooly racky sacky want some seafood, Mama!") was criticized by the first publisher, the *Atlantic Monthly*.[11] But the author's song of second choice draws together so well the various contrasts of the story—joy and pain, humor and fear, jazz music and blues tale—and it brings to a climax so well its important continuities—the excitement of constant movement and surprising complication, the symbolic suggestiveness of water and darkness, of eyes and mouth—that it seems, again, to be inevitable. Certainly it would be difficult to find a better illustration of Miss Welty's notions about the sometimes improvisational creation of stories, few of which are ever composed "in any typical, predictable, systematically developing, or even chronological way. . . . Each story . . . thrives in the course of being written only as long as it seems to have a life of its own" or of her sense of a good story's ultimate shape, "the beauty of order imposed, of structure rising and building upon itself, and finally of this coming to rest."[12]

Notes

[1] Numbers in parentheses refer to the text of "Powerhouse" in *The Collected Stories of Eudora Welty* (New York: Harcourt Brace Jovanovich, 1980).

[2] *A Season of Dreams: The Fiction of Eudora Welty* (Baton Rouge: Louisiana State University Press, 1965), 149.

[3] In analyzing several dozen references to water in the story, William Stone sees an image that "draws together Miss Welty's related themes of death, reality, Negritude and art," and he finds that Powerhouse especially "accepts water as his element, moves naturally in it, and thereby gains his strength—his power to overcome tragedy, and to produce his music"; see "Eudora Welty's Hydrodynamic 'Powerhouse,'" *Studies in Short Fiction* 11 (1974): 93-96.

[4] Appel observes that as

> a folk tradition, jazz has produced a handful of Negro musicians who have risen above the vast field of competition by virtue of their improvisatory skills, and, like the "Fast Guns" of the American West, have been acclaimed as virtual folk heroes by their peers and public. The great improvising jazzman—such as Lester Young or Charlie Parker—has become a minor romantic figure in our time; he has even inspired a modest "jazz literature." He is essentially a soloist rather than just a bandleader, for most bandleaders tend to be "Organization Men." He is a folk hero because he is an improviser rather than a dance band musician—an instinctual, emotional, on-the-spot creator who tries never to play the same solo twice, functioning in a society that attempts to inhibit the individual, to make him conform and "play the same solo" continually. The Negro bandleader Powerhouse is a soloist of this rank. (148)

See also observations on the "Powerhouse-Waller" style by Whitney Balliett in "Fats," *The New Yorker* 54 (April 10, 1978): 114-15.

[5] The case for Powerhouse as sad clown or, more specifically, as man of the blues is argued persuasively by Alfred Appel in his detailed analysis of the story in *A Season of Dreams*, 148-64; on the racial, marital, or artistic troubles that Powerhouse could be projecting here, see also Joseph Bryant, *Eudora Welty* (Minneapolis: University of Minnesota Press, 1968), 11; Marie-Antoinette Manz-Kung, *Eudora Welty* (Bern: Francke, 1971), 114; John Cooley, "Blacks as Primitives in Eudora Welty's Fiction," *Ball State University Forum* 14, iii (1973): 26-27; Stone, 96; Leroy Thomas, "Welty's 'Powerhouse,'" *Explicator* 36, iv (1978): 15-17; on white exploitation of black jazz, see especially,

Timothy Dow Adams, "A Curtain of Black: White and Black Jazz Styles in 'Powerhouse,'" *Notes on Mississippi Writers* 10 (1977): 57-61.

[6]There have been, from the beginning of the story, contrasts between certainty and uncertainty, between clear direction and disorder, with sentences and phrases like "It makes everyone crowd around. . . . This is absolute . . . he must know exactly" as opposed to "Is it possible that he could be this! . . . the end of human discipline . . . he himself seems lost." The uncertainty created by the Gypsy story and its sceptical reception by the sidemen is enlarged as the third section closes with the note of possible suicide ("If she went and killed herself!") as well as questions about the time and even the place. But the dominance of Powerhouse is also reinforced by his call for an intermission and his order to his men to follow him outside: "He is already at the back door, he has pulled it wide open, and with a wild, gathered up face is smelling the terrible night." (135)

[7]Adams suggests that Powerhouse and his men use the wordplay of black street language, particularly the rhymed response: "'Does you wish to touch him? Because he don't bite,' is rhymed with 'Now you got everything right.'" (pp. 58-59). He also mentions the possible use of "hidden language" called "signifying," which is discussed by Roger Abrahams, *Positively Black* (Englewood Cliffs: Prentice Hall, 1970), 40-41.

[8]See Smith Kirkpatrick, "The Anointed Powerhouse," *Sewanee Review* 77 (1969): 101-03.

[9]Elizabeth Evans, *Eudora Welty* (New York: Frederick Ungar, 1981), 146-47.

[10]Kirkpatrick, 107-08.

[11]Eudora Welty, *Eye of the Story*, 107-08, 143-44.

STAFFORD LIBRARY
COLUMBIA COLLEGE
COLUMBIA, MO 65216